THE WAY PEOPLE LIVE

Life Among the Indian Fighters

Titles in The Way People Live series include:

THE WAY
PEOPLE
LIVE

Life
Among the Indian
Fighters

by James P. Reger

Lucent Books, P.O. Box 289011, San Diego, CA 92198-9011

Library of Congress Cataloging-in-Publication Data

Reger, James P.
    Life among the Indian fighters / by James P. Reger.
        p.   cm. — (Way people live)
    Includes bibliographical references (p.   ) and index.
    ISBN 1-56006-349-1 (alk. paper)
    1. Pioneers—West (U.S.)—History—Juvenile literature.   2. Pioneers—
West (U.S.)—Biography—Juvenile literature. 3. Frontier and pioneer life—
West (U.S.)—Juvenile literature. 4. West (U.S.)—Biography—Juvenile litera-
ture. 5. Indians of North America—Wars—West (U.S.)—Juvenile literature.
I. Title.   II. Series.
F591.R419   1998
978—dc21   97-28776
                                                                                              CIP
                                                                                               AC

Copyright 1998 by Lucent Books, Inc., P.O. Box 289011, San Diego, California
92198-9011

Printed in the U.S.A.

Contents

Discovering the Humanity in Us All

The Way People Live series focuses on pockets of human culture. Some of these are current cultures, like the Eskimos of the Arctic; others no longer exist, such as the Jewish ghetto in Warsaw during World War II. What many of these cultural pockets share, however, is the fact that they have been viewed before, but not completely understood.

To really understand any culture, it is necessary to strip the mind of the common notions we hold about groups of people. These stereotypes are the archenemies of learning. It does not even matter whether the stereotypes are positive or negative; they are confining and tight. Removing them is a challenge that's not easily met, as anyone who has ever tried it will admit. Ideas that do not fit into the templates we create are unwelcome visitors—ones we would prefer remain quietly in a corner or forgotten room.

The cowboy of the Old West is a good example of such confining roles. The cowboy was courageous, yet soft-spoken. His time (it is always a he, in our template) was spent alternatively saving a rancher's daughter from certain death on a runaway stagecoach, or shooting it out with rustlers. At times, of course, he was likely to get a little crazy in town after a trail drive, but for the most part, he was the epitome of inner strength. It is disconcerting to find out that the cowboy is human, even a bit childish. Can it really be true that cowboys would line up to help the cook on the trail drive grind coffee, just hoping he would give them a little stick of pep-

permint candy that came with the coffee shipment? The idea of tough cowboys vying with one another to help "Coosie" (as they called their cooks) for a bit of candy seems silly and out of place.

So is the vision of Eskimos playing video games and watching MTV, living in prefab housing in the Arctic. It just does not fit with what "Eskimo" means. We are far more comfortable with snow igloos and whale blubber, harpoons and kayaks.

Although the cultures dealt with in Lucent's The Way People Live series are often historically and socially well known, the emphasis is on the personal aspects of life. Groups of people, while unquestionably affected by their politics and their governmental structures, are more than those institutions. How do people in a particular time and place educate their children? What do they eat? And how do they build their houses? What kinds of work do they do? What kinds of games do they enjoy? The answers to these questions bring these cultures to life. People's lives are revealed in the particulars and only by knowing the particulars can we understand these cultures' will to survive and their moments of weakness and greatness.

This is not to say that understanding politics does not help to understand a culture. There is no question that the Warsaw ghetto, for example, was a culture that was brought about by the politics and social ideas of Adolf Hitler and the Third Reich. But the Jews who were crowded together in the ghetto cannot be understood by the Reich's politics. Their life was a day-to-day battle for existence, and the creativity and methods they used to prolong their lives is a vital story of human perseverance that would be denied by focusing only on the institutions of Hitler's Germany. Knowing that children as young as five or six outwitted Nazi guards on a daily basis, that Jewish policemen helped the Germans control the ghetto, that children attended secret schools in the ghetto and even earned diplomas—these are the things that reveal the fabric of life, that can inspire, intrigue, and amaze.

Books in The Way People Live series allow both the casual reader and the student to see humans as victims, heroes, and onlookers. And although humans act in ways that can fill us with feelings of sorrow and revulsion, it is important to remember that "hero," "predator," and "victim" are dangerous terms. Heaping undue pity or praise on people reduces them to objects, and strips them of their humanity.

Seeing the Jews of Warsaw only as victims is to deny their humanity. Seeing them only as they appear in surviving photos, staring at the camera with infinite sadness, is limiting, both to them and to those who want to understand them. To an object of pity, the only appropriate response becomes "Those poor creatures!" and that reduces both the quality of their struggle and the depth of their despair. No one is served by such two-dimensional views of people and their cultures.

With this in mind, The Way People Live series strives to flesh out the traditional, two-dimensional views of people in various cultures and historical circumstances. Using a wide variety of primary quotations—the words not only of the politicians and government leaders, but of the real people whose lives are being examined—each book in the series attempts to show an honest and complete picture of a culture removed from our own by time or space.

By examining cultures in this way, the reader will notice not only the glaring differences from his or her own culture, but also will be struck by the similarities. For indeed, people share common needs—warmth, good company, stability, and affirmation from others. Ultimately, seeing how people really live, or have lived can only enrich our understanding of ourselves.

Boone: The Exemplar

Daniel Boone peered anxiously through the green-smelling foliage at five Shawnee braves cooking meat over an open fire. His fringed, buckskin shirt was black with sweat and his expression was more intense than any of five coonskin-capped companions had ever seen. That intensity did not surprise them, though. Wild-eyed and frightened themselves, they knew that this was not going to be a typical attack. These Indians had captured Boone's daughter and two other girls; Boone's party was here to get them back . . . alive.

That morning, Sunday, July 17, 1776, had begun like other Sunday mornings at the Boonesborough stockade in Kentucky. Work had ceased, the Bible had been read, and most of the men were inside their cabins taking naps. The sun-lulled peace exploded into mayhem, though, when a scream ripped up from the river below. Jolted awake, Boone recognized the voice immediately. It was Jemima, his precious fourteen-year-old. He had lost his son to Indians the year before and was instantly determined not to lose his daughter, too.

Jemima and two of her frolicking friends had drifted too far down the river in their canoe, unaware that they were being greedily eyed from the leafy shore. The girls represented a substantial trophy to the shock-haired braves watching them, strong young men in need of slaves, wives, and respect.

By the time Boone had bounded barefoot in his haste to the girls' canoe, the kidnappers had already disappeared deep into the black-green murk beneath the endless forest canopy. Catching up would require all of his skills as an Indian fighter. He would have to read the signs along trails and creeks, slowing his pace enough to find footprints, broken twigs, and any dropped clues that the girls might be leaving behind. Every squirrel that

Daniel Boone during the time he explored the wilderness of Kentucky.

Daniel Boone and companions rescue Boone's daughter and her friends from their Indian captors.

scurried, every rustling fern and trampled laurel bush would call his attention as would any human odors. He would have to differentiate every sound, smell, and sight and decide instinctively which was a potential ambush, which paths were false and which true, and how much time remained before the Shawnee wolves harmed his Jemima.

Three days and fifty slippery, sliding miles later, Boone and his companions found themselves in the bushes overlooking the Indians and their captives. Whatever they did next would determine whether the girls lived or died. It was up to Daniel. It always had been up to the chief scout and Indian fighter at moments like this. For as rugged and skillful as his coon-capped companions might have been as frontiersmen, they knew that they were at best still settlers and farmers. Only Boone was the professional Indian fighter, the wilderness scout. And they would happily defer to him.

At last, they saw his eyes steel over and his Pennsylvania long rifle, Old Tick-Licker, slowly rise to the ready. That was all the sign they needed. They waited tensely for Boone's first shot and, when it came, they let loose their own smoke, fire, and thunder and stormed screaming into the unsuspecting camp. Furiously, they drew back the butts of their discharged rifles to crush the Shawnees' skulls, but two of the braves were already writhing in their gunshot death throes and the others were running away. The fleeing Indians hurled back knives and tomahawks in vain. Only once did the fight come close to wounding a white person, when a charging settler mistook one of the girls for an Indian and nearly butted her face with his rifle. As quickly as they had attacked, they spun and fled, having saved the lives of three promising young women, snuffed out the lives of two promising young men, and added yet another adventure story to the growing legend of Daniel Boone.

One of Many

Boone's life not only serves as a singular example of the Indian fighter's courage and resourcefulness but as a model of what all

An illustration depicts a trapper and his dog. Such men spent months in the wilderness, trapping and gathering furs for trade.

Indian fighters of his era were like; how they survived, what they aspired to, and how they lived their daily lives. While no two Indian fighters (also known as scouts and frontiersmen) were exactly alike, a certain lifestyle evolved among them, which Daniel Boone exemplified, and that lifestyle included several distinct roles.

Since it was the beaver fur trade that initially brought the white man into contact with the Indians (and inevitably led to conflicts over the furs), the Indian fighters' first role was that of the fur trapper and trader. Very few early frontiersmen began their careers by stating that they wanted to be Indian fighters. Instead, these sturdy adventurers set out into the wilderness after the riches that pelts could bring them and became Indian fighters by necessity in a sort of "on-the-job training."

Either to open up untapped trapping grounds or to lead the growing number of pioneers into the heartland, trailblazing or road-building emerged as a second role requiring the particular skills of the Indian fighters. The reason is clear. The roads they endeavored to establish invariably ran through territory that had belonged to the Indians for generations. The natives' justifiable resistance to such trespassings often led to bloody fights.

Pioneer settlements eventually offered the Indian fighters their first truly professional role. Settlers began hiring men to do little else but range through the untamed lands near their settlements, scouting for Indian attacks and providing an early warning system of impending danger. This required the Indian fighters to take long, solitary treks among forested mountains reading signs and hunting game, which they often sold to the settlers whom they were charged with protecting. They often encountered Indian braves who were doing the same and engaged in perhaps the quintessential role of the Indian fighters: fighting Indians one-to-one in single warrior combat or in small groups.

As a result of these fights and the chases, captures, and tortures that often ensued, the unique philosophies and darkened attitudes of the Indian fighters evolved. Based on the Old Testament theology of an eye for an eye and a tooth for a tooth, they quickly grew to match the Indians vengeance for vengeance and atrocity for atrocity often without knowing or caring who had struck the first blow.

The deeper that Indian fighters and their families penetrated Indian territory, the more the braves raided their cabins and killed their wives and children. The Indian fighters visited the same horrors upon the Indian people with just as much brutality and vengeance. It was a constant war that raged atrociously between the two civilizations for generations, and neither side ever showed much mercy.

When large numbers of warriors, white and Indian, gathered on either side, full-scale battles often ensued. These battles sometimes involved uniformed armies, massive earthworks, and complex maneuvering. They also had far-reaching consequences to the growth of the American empire and the ultimate demise of the Indians. Within the context of these battles, other roles surfaced for the buckskin Indian fighters: scouting, sniping, night-fighting, and covert warfare techniques now associated with such elite groups as the U.S. Navy Seals and the Army Green Berets (units also known to have employed psychological operations often involving atrocities against their victims in time of war).

Although Indian fighters obviously got their names from fighting Indians, the enemy that claimed more of their lives than any other was nature. Between desert droughts

Indians decide the fate of their trapper captive. Both Indians and scouts visited brutalities upon each other as they competed for the same land and furs.

and freezing blizzards, poisonous snakes and buffalo stampedes, Indians were often the least of their concerns. It was the bear, though, both the eastern black bear and the western grizzly, that most terrified the Indian fighters; few of them ever reached maturity without several scars left by one or both of these awesome beasts.

Indeed, one of the most persistent stories passed down about Daniel Boone has him killing a bear with his long knife and then carving something like "D. Boon cilled A. Bar on tree" near the spot in Kentucky where the event is said to have taken place. Whether fact or lore, Boone held the mighty black bear in high esteem or his life would not have lasted long enough to represent the American Indian fighter as thoroughly as it did.

A Man Nearly from Birth

Even early in life Boone had caromed from one wilderness escapade to the next, enriched by a hands-on education that could not have better prepared him for frontier life. Born in Pennsylvania in 1734 to Quaker parents, he learned young to respect Indians and seek peaceful relations with them whenever possible. It was, in fact, the local natives who first taught him to track, hunt, and "think Indian."

By the age of ten, Boone was living alone in the woods caring for his father's cattle. At twelve, he was supplying meat for his family and trading hides for store-bought necessities. His father encouraged his son's long hunts in the forests, even though they lured him away from the classroom and seriously hindered his ability to read, write, "cipher" (learn basic arithmetic), and spell.

Young Boone's rebellious older brothers and sisters proved unable to live by the strict Quaker codes and, rather than censure his

children as Quaker law demanded, the elder Boone moved his entire family to untamed North Carolina. There in the far western reaches of the Yadkin River valley, hostile Indians hunted and conducted regular raids to stave off what they viewed as the white people's rape of their ancestral hunting grounds. Fifteen-year-old, "Indian thinking" Daniel Boone quickly gained even more respect and value both within his own family and among other settlers throughout the threatened area. However, his first chance to apply his knowledge of Indian warfare would not come for another four years.

First Blood Was Almost His

In 1755 the British were using the French and Indian War as a pretext to throw the French out of North America. British general Edward Braddock, a short, fat, and pompous man, headed a combined army of British redcoats and colonial Indian fighters (mostly young thrill seekers in buckskin like eighteen-year-old Daniel Boone). Braddock had orders to attack the French at Fort Duquesne, occupying the site that the British would later name Pittsburgh. Pigheadedly, Braddock refused to acknowledge the fighting abilities of his "undisciplined" frontiersmen and made wagon drivers out of them.

For that reason, among others, the French and their Indian allies routed the British, killed General Braddock, and sent young Boone and all others running for their lives. Boone returned home to North Carolina with nothing to show for his near-death experience but smarting pride, a disdain for generals, and a collection of what sounded to him like tall tales. There was a land, another teamster had told him, across the Appalachian Mountains, a lush, rolling land of forests, fields, and fish-

General Braddock, who foolishly believed his Indian foes were incompetent, lies dead after a 1755 battle during the French and Indian War.

rippled streams. Herds of buffalo, deer, and elk blackened the meadows there and shook the earth when they ran; flocks of turkey and other game birds thrived. The wagoneer called this fabled land Kentucky and said it was free for the taking if, of course, a man could find a pass to it through the mountains and, more importantly, wrench it from the Indians who had called it theirs for centuries.

A Dream Realized

Boone turned twenty-one and took a wife, a strong and pretty seventeen-year-old named Rebecca, but he never lost his fascination with the mythical paradise beyond the farthest blue-hazed ridge. Rebecca grew to know her husband's faraway eyes well and asked no questions when he finally announced, after ten years of mundane hunting and farming,

that he simply had to leave her and their several small children to find Kentucky and his dream.

Boone and a small party of men set out in 1769. Following an Indian trail along the Cumberland River, they eventually spilled down out of the mountains and into what seemed to be an echoing eternity of prehistoric forest floor stirring with wild animals. According to Boone's ghostwritten autobiography:

> We found everywhere an abundance of wild beasts of all sorts, through this vast forest. The buffaloes were more frequent than I have seen cattle in settlements, browsing on the leaves of the cane, or cropping the herbage on those extensive plains, fearless, because ignorant, of the violence of man. Sometimes we saw hundreds in a drove, and the numbers about

the salt springs were amazing. In this forest, the habitation of beasts of every kind natural to America, we practised hunting with great success.[1]

Hunter and Hunted

The party hunted for months, amassing a small fortune in furs and hides before the first of several encounters with Indians befell them. They had camped too near the trail one night, a mistake Boone would never again make, and a hunting party of Shawnee sprang on him and another man. The braves whirled their tomahawks and whooped soul-piercing cries but Boone kept his composure and, with effort, that of his panting partner. Remembering the disarming effect that good humor had had on the Indians he had known growing up, Boone began laughing and joking with the attackers as if they were old friends and finally managed to strike a deal: a trade of their hides for their freedom.

Boone proved to be as tenacious as he was brave, however, and doubled back to pursue the hides' new owners. While the Indians slept that fire-embered night, he and his friend crept into camp and stole back their horses and hides. They kicked the horses to a hard ride in spite of being pummeled in the darkness by low branches and rocky outcroppings. But when the cold, misty morning finally dawned, they had to rest themselves and the horses. It was then that the Indians snared them again.

Some Very Serious "Fun"

Escape the third time, Boone knew, would not be so easy. He later recalled, "The time of our sorrow was now arrived and the scene fully opened. The Indians plundered us of what we had, and kept us in confinement for seven days, treating us with common savage usage. We were then in a dangerous, helpless situation, exposed daily to perils and death among savages, not a white man in the country but ourselves."[2]

Undaunted, he simply began spreading the frontier charm more thickly. For several days and nights, he slapped backs and roared his sparkling laughter. He acted out stories around campfires and dazzled his audience with his dancing blue eyes. Before long he was as much a guest as a prisoner, though he knew that he could not just walk away with a wave and a smile. Nevertheless, the Indians did loosen their watch on him more with each passing night until he and his companion could melt away into the succoring darkness.

Boone stayed on in "Kaintuck" for another year, five months of which he spent entirely alone. He mused of that interlude:

> In spite of being many hundred miles from my beloved family, I believe few would have equally enjoyed the happiness I experienced. I was surrounded by plenty in the midst of want. I was happy in the midst of dangers and inconveniences. In such diversity it was impossible I should be disposed to melancholy. No populous city, with all the varieties of commerce and stately structures, could afford so much pleasure to my mind, as the beauties of nature I found there.[3]

A More Seasoned Young Man

Boone now slept far from the paths, often building deceptive campfires miles from his true lair. To disguise his trail, he padded through stony creek beds and even swung like a monkey from vine to branch to limb. He masked the telltale scent of his own sweat and oils with urine from the elk and buffalo and always sniffed for the musky scents of other humans.

He took on Indians only twice during his solitude, the first time when he shot a brave in the back from a long distance, supposedly because he could not tell whether his victim had spotted him, and he dared not risk that he had. During the other encounter, Indians cornered him on a cliff some sixty feet above the forest canopy (and another sixty past that to the bouldered ground) and closed in, grinning, for the capture or kill. But Boone whirled around and charged full speed straight off the precipice, shocking himself as well as his pursuers by landing safely in the leafy cushion of the summer maple trees.

Boone returned home to North Carolina in 1771, but not before Indians again robbed him of his hides. So, after two years away

Fickle Fame

Only one man could truthfully boast, "I made Daniel Boone famous." And that man was a highly unlikely figure. He was a scrawny, bumbling schoolmaster from Pennsylvania named John Filson, and he possessed none of the skills required for surviving in the wilderness. But he did know how to write.

Enduring endless frontier pranks, swindles, and crude indignities, the thirty-year-old "squarehead" from back East pursued his goal with the industriousness of a beaver. That goal was to increase the value of the Kentucky lands in which he had invested by writing a book on the glories of wilderness living. As part of his project, he interviewed Daniel Boone, well known then only in Kentucky, and ghostwrote the oral ramblings of the semiliterate frontiersman as *The Autobiography of Daniel Boone*.

Though Boone always claimed that the content of his "autobiography" was accurate, he would have been hard pressed, atrocious speller that he was, to defend the literary voice as truly his own. The man who supposedly celebrated his victory over a bear by carving "D. Boon cilled A. Bar on tree" would have had a hard time convincing readers that he had written a passage this formal and flowery:

> I surveyed the famous river Ohio that rolled in silent dignity, marking the western boundary of Kentucky with inconceivable grandeur. At a vast distance, I beheld the mountains lift their venerable brows, and penetrate the clouds. All things were still. I returned to my family with a determination to bring them as soon as possible to live in Kentucke, which I esteemed a second paradise, at the risk of my life and fortune.

Filson's *Autobiography* had to some degree the desired effect. The book sold well at first and did temporarily increase the demand for and, hence, the value of Kentucky land. And it elevated Daniel Boone to national recognition. The initial wave of interest passed, however, and the Indians killed John Filson before he could reap any monetary gains from his real estate investment. The book took on new life in Europe, though, a few years after Boone's own death, finally according him international celebrity that has never faded.

from his wife and children, he had very little to show for his efforts. He was not discouraged, though. He continued to believe that Kentucky would be the source of his riches, and he burned inside to take his family there to live. Mounting one expedition of settlers to cross through the mountains in 1773, he turned it back after a personal tragedy. Indians captured and slow-tortured his son and another young man to a grinding, grisly death.

A Settlement at Last . . . and Another Capture

In 1775 a judge and land speculator named Richard Henderson hired Boone and others to blaze a new trail through the Cumberland Gap into Kentucky, a trail wide enough to accommodate wagons. Henderson intended to establish his own colony in the wilderness and needed this road, the Wilderness Road, over which to move his "colonists."

The colony never materialized, but three stockade settlements did: Harrodsburg, Logan's Fort, and, in honor of the man who had done the most to get them there, Boonesborough. And almost as soon as the last palisade log had been sharpened and cabin roof shingled, the Indians began their attacks, in small groups at first, targeting people working beyond the gates, but soon attacking the stockade itself.

In 1778 Boone led a party of thirty Boonesborough men to boil down salt from a distant saline spring. Shawnee braves captured him when he was off hunting by himself and forced him to guide the braves back to the other white men. Eventually, the Indians released most of Boone's men, but they kept their prize catch, Daniel Boone himself. After making him "run the gauntlet" (being savagely beaten while running through a tunnel of weapon-thrashing men and women), the Shawnee dubbed him Big Turtle and the chief made him his own son.

Daniel Boone points to the unexplored beauty of Kentucky. Boone, who dreamed of settling the wild land, lost his son to the Indians during his explorations.

Boone Saves Another

At least one other man benefited by Daniel Boone's escapes from the Shawnee. An Indian fighter from what is now West Virginia, one Martin Wetzel, had escaped in like fashion after two and a half years of captivity and stumbled into the Boonesborough stockade. Looking more like an Indian than a white man, he could not convince the Boonesborough settlers that he was indeed one of them. The fact that he claimed to have come from an Indian village known to have been destroyed by whites years earlier did not help validate his story. According to Allan W. Eckert's *That Dark and Bloody River*, the exchange went like this:

> "Don't shoot!" Wetzel cried. "I'm a white man! Don't shoot!"
>
> One of the sentries fired but missed.
>
> He hit the ground shouting, "For God's sakes, don't shoot! I'm white! I've just escaped from the Shawnees!"
>
> Wetzel pleaded that the Indian village he claimed to have escaped from had been rebuilt and was again populated, but the sentries did not believe him. Daniel Boone appeared and Wetzel told his story to him.
>
> After carefully considering it, Boone laughed and said, "Well, boys, I don't find anything at all improbable 'bout what he says. There ain't no doubt in my mind that he is who he says he is and that things've happened the way he's told 'em. Better let 'im go."
>
> "Still think we ort'a kill'im," someone muttered.
>
> "Would you've wanted to kill me when I got away from 'em?" Boone asked. "If you're gonna kill white captives who escape from the Injens, that sure ain't gonna be much encouragement for others t'try t'get away."

At that, the sentries relented, thereby adding another man's name to the long list of those saved by Daniel Boone.

For several months, Boone lived the Indian life, loving everything about it except the separation from his family. He might have stayed there much longer, hunting and whooping and having shooting matches with his new "brothers," had he not heard them laying plans to attack Boonesborough.

Paul Revere of the Wilderness

Boone finally bolted away on a bareback horse while the braves were out hunting turkey; he drove the animal relentlessly throughout the night until it collapsed beneath him and died in a rocky creek bed. Running almost nonstop for four days and nights, he covered 160 miles and arrived at Boonesborough to find it broken down and indefensible. He immediately put the settlers to work rebuilding the stockade and increasing the number of blockades to four. Chopping and burning trees near the fort, they denied the Indians cover until at last the fort was as ready as it could be. Then the anxious waiting began, but no Indians appeared, so Boone and a party set out to scout their whereabouts.

Boone found the Shawnee soon enough, five hundred of them in the company of

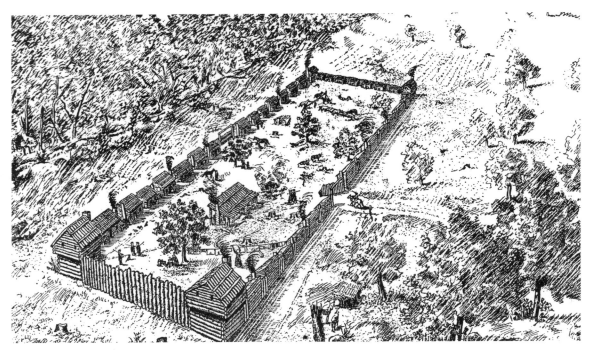

The plan of the Boonesborough fort during its heyday. The fort withstood a ten-day siege by the Shawnee in 1778.

British agents. During his Shawnee captivity, Boone had stalled these agents from attacking the settlement by professing that he and all of Boonesborough would go over to the British side in the Revolutionary War. He made his true intentions clear, though, when he had his scouting party snipe and hatchet away at the war party as it approached. Not even peace talks with his Indian "father" could sway Daniel's conviction to stand and fight but the "palaverin" (parley) did stall the Indians long enough to allow the settlers to store up food, powder, water, and bullets. The talks broke off, however, and the Indians' siege began.

From Skirmishing to Battling

For over a week the Indians laid siege to the stockade, blasting away with their rifles.

Snipers took hilltop positions surrounding the fort and wounded several settlers by firing down into it. A white settler hiding in the woods said that at one point,

> The Indians made in the night a dreadful attack on the fort. They run up, a large number of them with large firebrands or torches, and made the most dreadful screams and hollering that could be imagined. I heard the Indians killing people and heard the women and children and men also screaming when the Indians was killing them.[4]

They set fire to the wooden walls and gleefully watched them burn, but a fortuitous downpour quenched the flames to hissing smoke. Frustrated by the failure of their conventional assault, the Shawnee burrowed a tunnel under the palisade that another providential rainfall caused to collapse.

Ten days of siege, however, had exhausted the settlers and their supplies. They had no ammunition, powder, food, or water and the moaning wounded provided a demoralizing backdrop. Some talked of surrender, others of trying to break out. But the point became moot when the Indians, inexplicably convinced that the settlers could hold out indefinitely, gave up and went home.

And so ended the Boonesborough Siege of 1778, the closest the Indians ever came to significantly delaying the encroachment of Daniel Boone and his followers on their Kaintuck-ee. It would take a force far more corrupt and insidious to sweep a man like Boone off of his claimed landholdings. It would take a band of eastern lawyers to exploit the fact that he had failed to obtain the right kind of title to his hard-won lands and the court system, with the slam of a gavel, to render him penniless.

In his later years, Boone enjoyed fame but not fortune in West Virginia and Missouri. Lawyers connived to strip him of his landholdings there, too, leaving the legendary Indian fighter to die at eighty-five without a cent to show for his struggles. Nevertheless, he died happy in the knowledge that he had inspired two generations of American frontiersmen to grapple to the death with the Indians for the resources and the land that would make America great. And chief among those resources was the beaver.

CHAPTER 1

Furs and Fortunes: The First Grounds for Conflict

What was it about fur trapping that could drive men who had barely survived unspeakable hardships to plunge right back into the wilderness cauldron all over again? Was it the excitement, the adventure, the solitude, the closeness to nature? It was probably all of these things and more, but foremost among motivators was simply money. There was a profit to be made in the pelts of beavers, sometimes a huge profit, even for the "lowly" trappers themselves. Indeed, the possibility existed for a few industrious men to begin their lives in buckskin and end them in the costliest of tailored fabrics.

When such men did manage to effect that metamorphosis, fashion required that they own several hats made of the beaver pelts like those they had once cut from the plump, paddle-tailed rodents. These were no ordinary fur hats, though, in the banal tradition of frontier coonskin caps. These were high-crowned, felt top hats as sleek and elegant as any made of oriental silk.

Regardless of what drove it, the fur trade presented white men with one of the first reasons to establish contact with the North American Indians. That contact often led to conflict and, hence, the two centuries of violence be-

A frontiersman attempts to trade liquor for food with a skeptical Indian. The settlers' introduction of liquor to the Indians created anger and resentment among the tribes.

tween them that followed. Once the Indians learned that they could trade their furs for steel tomahawks, liquor, knives, cloth, copper pots, and firearms, the competition for the beaver began, and so did the battling. In response, men who had begun as fur trappers and traders took on a new name: Indian fighters. Soon, the two groups were at war and legends of survival were born; legends like that of John Colter and his run to escape the Blackfeet.

Marathon John

Fur trapper John Colter sprinted, naked and bloody, across the high plains of Wyoming. The year was 1807 and he had just resigned from the Lewis and Clark expedition to find his fortune trapping the abundant beaver. But Indians had captured him and forced him to run, unclothed, like prey for their sporting pleasure. Panting and wheezing, he shot panicked glimpses over his shoulder, dismayed to see eight hundred Blackfoot warriors keeping up their whooping pursuit. He dashed and leaped with remarkable agility for a man of thirty-five, especially one who was continually slashing his bare feet and legs on spiny prickly-pear cacti.

Huffing their way across one mile, two miles, three miles, and then four, the most determined braves began to close within spear-chucking range. With the almost supernatural power that terror alone can produce, Colter ignored his burning, cramping muscles and turned on even more speed. It cost him, though, for blood started gushing up from his heaving lungs and shot out of his nostrils. Finally, he managed to pull away from all of the Indians, all except one, who doggedly refused to yield.

According to the man who first heard him recount his ordeal,

Trapper John Colter sits in the wilderness with his dog. Colter often trapped alone in Blackfoot territory, sometimes barely escaping with his life.

Colter had now arrived within a mile of the river, when he distinctly heard the appalling sound of footsteps behind him, and every instant expected to feel the spear of his pursuer. Again he turned his head, and saw the savage not twenty yards from him. Determined if possible to avoid the expected blow, he suddenly stopped, turned around, and spread out his arms. The Indian, surprised by the suddenness of the action and perhaps of the bloody appearance of Colter, also attempted to stop; but exhausted with running, he fell whilst endeavoring to throw his spear, which stuck in the ground and broke in his hand. Colter instantly snatched up the pointed part.[5]

Thus Spake the Indian Fighters

Fur trappers and Indian fighters took pride in being a breed unto themselves. They cast off every eastern "corncracker's" convention, starting with the way they spoke. Color in language meant everything to the trappers; the less they used "flatlander" talk the better. Had these bawdy men grown up as learned poets, their richly descriptive metaphors and similes would have been lauded by the literary mainstream. As it was, they happily purpled the air with their ribald epithets and "palavered" as it suited them.

When in need of whiskey, they cried out for baldface or a jack of likker or maybe a swig of panner piss or a take of the horn. If it was a smoke they wanted, they asked for baccer or backy or honeydew or a taste of Ol' Virginny. Few pleasures surpassed strapping on the feedbag after a hard day's work and nothing satisfied like buffler (buffalo) unless of course they could get boudie (buffalo intestines). Otherwise they would have to eat pemmican again, dried meat and berries pounded together with melted fat and stored in cakelike rations.

If it was an Indian fight the trappers were after, they might say that they were half starved for hair and wanted to black their faces and shoot Galena pills into them (bullets made with lead from Galena, Illinois). Perhaps they would speak of tickling Indians' humpribs with a 'hawk or make meat of them by wading into their livers with knives.

In more peaceful times, they might find a robe warmer to take for a wife and maybe even birth a few pups. She could keep the fire punched up during robe season and provide some right shinin' times. Of course, they always had to keep a look out for Old Ephraim, a bear. It took plenty of pluck to make meat out of a bear and the same stood true for a panner cat, a panther.

Whatever the creature, place, item, or activity, the Indian fighters had a phrase for it that probably evoked more understanding within the listener than any pretentious prose of the day. And if no phrase existed, they simply made one up so apt it rarely needed explanation.

Reacting in pure animal rage, he rammed the spear point completely through the writhing brave's gut and pinned him to the ground until his agony gave way to the stillness of death. Sagging over his kill only long enough to regain some remnant of his labored breath, he wrenched the point out. He could hear the rest of the warriors approaching, their howls renewing his craving to live, so he pulled himself up and ran on until he reached a small river.

Diving underwater before any pursuers could see him, he came up for air in an abandoned beaver lodge. He silenced his gasping and peered out through the cracks just as the main body of Blackfeet came into view along the bank. In minutes, they were swarming over his refuge but they were unable to find it. Colter watched and listened as the red-orange dusk and the war whoops gradually faded into the black, silent night.

The trapper lay there, wet, exhausted, and shivering, until the last of the Indians moved on. Then he slipped out of the water and resumed his odyssey of survival. Without food, clothing, weapons, or potable water, he set out for the nearest fur trapping post 350 miles away. He ate roots, made "blankets" of dirt under which to sleep, and navigated by the sun and the stars. Eleven days later, he stumbled, half dead, into the post. It took him only two weeks to heal before he headed back out to the same trapping grounds from which he had just escaped.

It Takes Two

In fairness to the Indians, a question needs to be asked regarding the events that led up to such violent encounters. What did the frontier fur trappers and traders do in their dealings with the Indians in the first place to cause the distrust and unmitigated wrath of so many tribes in both the East and the West?

For one, endless numbers of broken treaties and the invasion of whites over their

hunting, ceremonial, and traditional homelands aggravated the Indians.

Germs, Innocence, and Guilt

The fur-trapping Indian fighters were responsible for many other more subtle forms of oppression, the worst of which, epidemic diseases, was mostly unwitting. The white men could carry the viruses of such potentially devastating sicknesses as smallpox, measles, and pneumonia without becoming ill themselves because they had been exposed to them in the white culture for years and gradually developed immunities to them. The Indians, however, had no such immunities to

An Indian asserts his land rights by refusing to let a wagon train pass through his territory. Indian tribes soon realized that the whites would never stop taking their land.

what were, to them, new virulent strains and they died by the millions as a result.

While nearly every Indian's death from the frontiersmen's diseases was unintentional, most Indians bitterly held them responsible nonetheless; in part because of one utterly atrocious act of barbarism. In 1764, Colonial English general Sir Jeffrey Amherst wrote this damning order to one of his frontier officers: "Could it not be contrived to send the small pox among our disaffected tribes of Indians? You will do well to try to inoculate the Indians by means of blankets, as well as to try every other method that can serve to extirpate this execrable race."[6]

The treachery worked. Shawnee and Delaware Indians sieging Fort Pitt, Pennsylvania, accepted the infected blankets as gifts from the frontiersmen during a "peace talk." The resulting epidemic wiped the warriors out in the worst kind of way—with grinding aches, shivering fevers, and rashes of pimples that swelled into bursting boils. Again, however, this intentional act of Indian fighter savagery appears to have been isolated, but its effects on white/Indian relations were not.

As If They Needed More Reasons to Hate

Regardless of intentionality, though, the human effects of contact with the frontiersmen were crippling to the Indian cultures, and the Indians increasingly held the whites responsible. One historian noted the damage, writing, "Indians changed from hunters to commercial gatherers of ever-increasing quantities of pelts and hides to meet their expanding tastes for trade goods (from the Indian fighters). This growing dependence on manufactured goods destroyed Indian self-sufficiency, causing personal and social disorientation and decay. Saturation trapping and hunting over his range soon destroyed the wild creatures that had provided him with food, shelter, and clothing. He and his tribe were reduced to a state of poverty not of his making."[7]

Neither did the Indians cause many of the wars they eventually had to fight with their neighboring tribes. As the fur trade exhausted the supply of beavers and other game from their own lands, they had to move farther west into the lands of nearby tribes to "poach" their furs. Conflict was inevitable between these previously noninteracting tribes, and it was exacerbated by the violently competitive French and English trappers who further incited them against each other in order to gain allies for their own wars.

A Double-Edged Blade

The perils involved when Indian fighters and Indians interacted were not one-sided, however. They were obvious when Indian fighters encountered hostile Indians in battle. But what about the contact with the many tribes that were either allied with frontiersmen or neutral and offered them friendship, sanctuary, and even membership in the tribe? Could there have been dangers there, too? A misguided early historian, speaking for a majority of eighteenth- and nineteenth-century whites, thought so, and he "exposed" the so-called ill-effects of such friendly comingling on the Indian fighters. In so doing, however, he inadvertently captured much of the essence of who the Indian fighters really were.

At first, great hopes were entertained that, by the mingling of whites and Indians, the latter would be won over to civilization and Christianity; but the effect was precisely the reverse, because rather

A wandering trapper with his Indian wife. Many trappers became so fond of the wilderness lifestyle that they never returned to white society.

than the Indians becoming white, the whites became Indians. These outflowings of white civilization were merged in the waste of barbarism, as a river is lost in the sands of the desert. The wandering trapper chose a wife or a concubine among his Indian friends, and in a few generations, scarcely a tribe was free from an infusion of Celtic blood.

The fur trade engendered a peculiar class of men who shook loose every tie of blood and kindred and identified themselves with the Indians. Throughout the wilderness, the traveler would have encountered men owning the blood and speaking the language of the whites, yet, in their wild and swarthy visages and barbarous costume, seeming more akin to those with whom they had cast their lot.

The renegade of civilization caught the habits and imbibed the prejudices of his chosen associates. He loved to decorate his long hair with eagle feathers and make his face hideous with vermillion, ochre, and soot. In his wilderness dwelling, he lounged on a bearskin while his wife boiled his venison and lit his pipe. In hunting, in dancing, in singing, in taking a scalp, he rivalled the genuine Indian.[8]

And he learned so much from the Indian about how to survive in the wild.

Traversing the Wilderness Highways

Because no roads and few trails linked the mountain forests and thicketed prairies of the American wilderness, Indians and their "students," the trappers, relied upon the most ancient network of natural passageways: the lakes, streams, and rivers. One of the most

Mandan women carry bullboats on a journey along the Missouri River. White scouts copied the design of these ingenious boats.

widely used boats employed a design learned from the Indians. Trappers called it a bullboat because the massive skins of the bull buffalo formed the waterproof hull. Stretching the hide or hides over a bowl-shaped frame of bendable willow branches, the bullboat proved to be a roomy, relatively stable craft that could bob down even the most whitewatered of rivers. The waterborne trappers could patch leaks with tallow or bear grease and even heavily damaged bullboats sank slowly enough to allow riders to safely offload their cargos, often a ton or more of furs, traps, men, and supplies. Said one trapper of his bullboat: "Here we made three bullboats of buffalo bull's skins, sewing together two skins for each boat, then stretching them over a frame. Our boat contained three men, about sixty steel traps, five hundred beaver skins, our guns, and ammunition, besides other commodities."[9]

Log rafts took longer to make since they required the felling and stripping of trees plus the additional notching, similar to that used when constructing log cabins, required to interlock them. Powered and steered by long poles, rafts could reliably transport great loads of furs and supplies over calm waters but portaging them, carrying them over and around rapids, proved next to impossible due to their cumbersome weight. Some raft builders proved better than others: Fur trader Zenas Leonard seems to have taken a few too many shortcuts.

"Supposing the Indians were not so numerous on the other side of the river," Leonard wrote, "I resolved to cross over—for which purpose I built a raft of old logs, laid my shot, pouch gun, blanket, etc. on it, and pushed for the opposite shore. But my raft hit a rock and came apart, leaving me defenseless in the wilderness for several weeks."[10]

Dugouts, hewn logs with the insides scooped out, enjoyed popularity among Indian-fighting hunters and trappers due to their lighter weight and maneuverability both in the water and on portages. However, they required the skillful use of specialty tools such as awls and adzes in their construction and generally transported less poundage than bullboats or rafts.

In the eastern woodlands where birch trees were abundant, Indian fighters preferred the lightest and most swift of all Indian watercraft: the birch bark canoe. By stitching together wide strips of the naturally waterproof bark of birch trees with rawhide strings or spruce roots, one could fashion a tight, long-lasting skin on a sleek frame of cedar branches. The result was a hydrodynamically efficient vessel capable of transporting large cargos at white-capping speeds. The design was destined to become an enduring symbol of both the American Indians and the European-Americans who fought them. One old man boasted of his adventures as a canoe man:

> No portage was too long for me. I could carry, paddle, walk, and sing with any man I ever saw. When others stopped to carry at a bad step and lost time, I pushed on— over rapids, over cascades, over chutes;

Indian Women and Wives

It was not unusual for a welcoming chief or prominent brave to offer a trapper one of his wives free of charge for a night or two as a way of sweetening a pending fur-trading deal. If the trapper took a liking to the woman (more often than not because of her capacity to cook, camp, and carry heavy loads), the husband might sell her to the white man as a slave or wife, depending on how the trapper came to regard her. Such a transaction must have been degrading and depersonalizing for the Indian woman but was a reasonable alternative to the overwork, the beatings, and the general disrespect she likely suffered as the third or fourth wife of a brave. Being the only woman of a white man, however cruel in his own right, was at least no worse than the life to which she was accustomed.

Some Indian slave-wives were fortunate enough to continue living in their home villages if their trapping husbands chose to "go Indian" and settle down there. The French-Canadian trapper Toussaint Charbonneau bought a Shoshoni woman and lived with her in her village until a pair of white explorers hired them both as scouts, translators, and guides. The explorers were Meriwether Lewis and William Clark. The slave-wife called herself Bird Woman, or, in Shoshoni, Sacajawea.

Whites unfamiliar with frontier ways often frowned upon the "unholy unions" within the villages and the way they tended to make the whites more like the Indians than the other way around. One sanctimonious critic is quoted in Longtrail Snowbird's *The Alliances Between White Traders, Trappers, and Indian Women:*

> We found in this village a white man who has resided among the Indians for upwards of fourteen years, has a wife and family who dress and live like the natives. He retains the outward appearance of a Christian but his principles are much worse than those of the Indians. He is possessed of every superstition natural to those people as well as every dirty trick associated with the scoundrels.

It should be noted that a great number of those "scoundrels" died as a result of the venereal diseases that the white Christians introduced to Indian villages.

all were the same to me. No water, weather, ever stopped the paddle or the song. I beat all Indians at the race, and no white man ever passed me in the chase. And now I have not a spare shirt to my back, nor a penny to buy one. Yet, were I young again, I should glory in commencing the same career again.[11]

A Man's Home

Indian fighters and trappers also borrowed heavily from the Indians when it came time to bed down for the night. During the warmer months, they preferred to sleep under the stars, wrapped in a blanket beneath a buffalo robe. They sometimes added a little comfort by fashioning a mattress of leaves or pine boughs, resting their heads on a saddle or a second blanket. Always, they kept their weapons and moccasins close by in case a midnight dash for safety might be required.

On wintry nights, trappers often constructed a small hut like those used by the Indians for centuries. They wove a dome-shaped frame of strong but flexible willow branches and draped it with the ever-useful buffalo robe. In blizzards, they enclosed themselves completely within the dome hut, but whenever weather permitted, they built fires just outside an open flap. During more temperate months, they often used another Indian design, described by the inveterate trapper and Indian fighter Jedediah Smith:

Scouts arrive at an Indian encampment in birch bark canoes similar to those used by the Indians.

Tracking, trapping, gutting, skinning, scraping, drying, packing, and transporting beaver pelts contributed only partly to the success of a trapper's season, for if he was unable to sell his pelts to a fur trader his efforts in the wilderness amounted to nothing. In the eastern woodlands of Kentucky, Tennessee, and other areas of the Appalachians, fur trading posts sprang up along the edge of the frontier that were relatively easy for trappers to reach whenever their mules could carry no more. The Rocky Mountains of the West, however, covered such vast territory that trappers ready to sell their furs sometimes found distant trading posts were out of reach.

In 1825 officials of the American Trading Company devised a solution: They would bring the fur traders to the trappers. They began spreading the word months in advance that their buyers would meet trappers at a location chosen to be as convenient to all concerned as possible. They called their event a "rendezvous," French for "meeting."

For the next fifteen to twenty years, the rendezvous came to offer the trappers, Indian fighters, and many Indians as well an annual opportunity to sell their pelts, buy the next year's supplies, and socialize in ways that they had been craving over the past year

of solitude. And when these robust men socialized, they did so with vigor.

They drank, cussed, fist fought, wrestled, raced horses, and paid Indian men for a night with their wives. They bet on tomahawk throws, rifle shooting, and a simple game called hands wherein they wagered on which of another man's hands was holding a stone. Once they had purchased supplies for the year ahead, the trappers spent their surplus for the past year as if it did not mean much. After all, there was no place to spend it where they were going. So the buckskin ruffians threw their money away on whiskey, women, and childish games of chance. One witness, quoted in George Ruxton's *Ruxton of the Rockies*, reported:

> The rendezvous is one continued scene of drunkenness, gambling, and brawling, and fighting, as long as the money and credit of the trappers lasts. These annual gatherings are often the scene of bloody duels, for over their cups and cards no men are more quarrelsome than your mountaineers. Rifles at twenty paces, settle all differences.

One would think that even a day or two of such splendid peril might have satisfied these raucous men, but no, the "ronnyvoo" often went on for a month.

When not in winter, the lodges are about three feet high and are made up of forks and poles covered with grass weeds. As the rainy season approaches dirt is thrown on the roof to give it a slope to carry off the water and also secure the sides with dirt leaving only a small aperture for a door. When several shelters are thus built, the men camping build small fires

between them. When they become cold they draw the sand out from under the fires and spread it where they sleep.[12]

Fire: The Sustainer of Life

Most trapping Indian fighters arrived on the frontier with their own established methods

The Forgotten Slave Trade

The scourge of the African slave trade has long dominated the discussion of human bondage in America but the accursed institution existed on the continent long before any Europeans appeared. American Indians considered slavery a well-woven thread in the fabric of their lives and practiced it with equal parts acceptance and cruelty. Tribes with languages, customs, religions, and sensibilities as diverse as those presently existing between, for example, China and the United States routinely raided and warred with each other, often for the sole purpose of capturing slaves. Few grown men were considered "breakable," so they were usually tortured to death; still impressionable children and women, on the other hand, were valuable commodities to buy and sell.

As is the rationale wherever slavery exists, the Indian enslavers considered the cultures from which they snatched their victims inferior. It is interesting to note that nearly every tribe had a word for themselves that translated roughly as "the human beings." Implicit in such a name is the judgment that all others not belonging to their tribe were something less than human. With prejudices as deeply ingrained as those, it is understandable that the various Indian tribes felt no compunction in robbing other Indians of their freedom.

As Spanish, French, and British Indian fighters began exploiting the continent, it seemed only natural for them to join in the established slave trade, especially when searching for pretty, hardworking women with whom to spend the cold nights of winter. One trapper took part in a bloody raid by the Crows against their ancient enemy, the Blackfeet, solely to capture women for the slave market. They were not disappointed with their quarry. As quoted in *Ruxton of the Rockies*, the trapper wrote:

> We marched the women to an open piece of ground, made them form a line, and proceeded to make a selection. The aged and ill-favored, and the numerous matrons we withdrew from the body, telling them to return to the village and depart without clamor. They went away in sullenness, with their eyes flashing fire. The remainder, to the number of fifty-nine, very attractive looking young women, we carried along with us.

It is little wonder that the Indian fighters considered black African slavery to be entirely acceptable.

An Indian takes captive a woman from another tribe. The woman will no doubt be destined for a life of slavery.

A trapper surveys a stream for the presence of beavers. Trappers laid the traps directly in knee-deep water.

of starting fires. They struck something akin to brass knuckles made of steel against pieces of flint, creating sparks that ignited tinder, bark, or twists of dry grass, or else they used little magnifying glasses to focus sunlight into incendiary rays. Both the steel flint strikers and the "burning glasses" also doubled as highly desired trade items when dealing with friendly Indians, who soon made them a part of their technology.

But when white men found themselves without the resources for either method, they had to rely upon the ancient Indian technique of using a bow and fireboard. Starting a fire this way required five things: a small bow, a fireboard with a coin-size hole through it, a foot-long stick called a spindle, a hand block with a notch in its center, and volumes of patience. Those successful at starting a fire this way wrapped the bowstring around the spindle, secured one end of the spindle in the notched hand block and the other end snug-

gly in the fireboard hole, and sawed back and forth until the friction ignited the tinder in the fireboard hole. Most trappers did not even attempt to invest the number of hours required to master this technique, but they considered "sawing up a fire" a good backup skill with which they should at least be familiar.

The Trappers' Reason for Being

Once such "household" matters as transportation, shelter, and fire were worked out, the Indian-fighting trappers could settle down to their raison d'être, their reason for being, which was trapping beavers. The initial task for the trappers was to locate a promising spot where the slick-furred rodents might congregate. The first white men who came into the wilderness saw so many beavers cloying the waters as to render skillful detection unnecessary. As the animal population declined, however, well-kept lodges and dams in streams provided needed evidence of recent beaver activity, as did freshly gnawed-down trees and stumps along the banks.

As soon as they found a likely spot, the trappers waded knee-deep into the frigid water with one of their six or eight steel traps and a pole. They pounded the pole into the creek bed with a rock, spread the spring-loaded trap jaws apart with their feet, and very carefully reached down and clicked the weight-sensitive pan into its notched position. They then secured the trap to the pole with a length of chain and baited it.

The bait, or "medicine," came from the Indians, who had been trapping beavers with woven-stick traps for centuries. They had long ago discovered that the scent from the glands located near the anus of beavers excited, stimulated, and attracted the animals from as far as a mile away. Capitalizing on this Indian know-how, the white trappers always carried a pouch of the yellow urine-based goo, called castoreum (castor was another name for beaver), which they placed above the waterline on a separate, smaller stick.

The beavers would investigate the pungent aroma, resting a webbed foot on the pan in order to stretch up for a closer, upward sniff, and their leg would be caught and broken by the traps' unleashed jaws. Held beneath the water, the furry animals would drown before they could gnaw off their broken legs and escape.

After treating themselves to the delicacy of roasted beaver tail, the trappers would cut, gut, and scrape the flesh from inside the skins. They would then sew the pelts onto a circular willow-branch frame and hang them up to dry. When an area was trapped out and the valuable pelts were cinched onto the back of a mule, the trappers had to focus on becoming Indian fighters again. For as the growing weight of furs sagged on the backs of the pack animals, the white men represented an ever more valuable prize to any Indians they might encounter. They always resolved not to give up the fruits of six months' or a year's labor without negotiating to keep most of it. And if such negotiations failed, they were prepared to grapple with the Indians to the doors of death, making them the greatest practical Indian fighters of the age.

Trailblazers in the East

CHAPTER 2

Trailblazers in the East

During the eighteenth century, the eastern woodlands blanketed the American continent from the Atlantic Ocean to the Mississippi River with a thick, unbroken tangle of evergreen and deciduous forests, vines, shrubs, and a nearly impenetrable thicket of ground cover. The only way to travel through that jungle of foliage was by boat or by walking alongside the rivers and streams. The problem with that was that a person could go only where the waterways allowed him to go. It was, therefore, considered an amazing breakthrough any time trailblazers and road builders cut down enough trees to establish an overland passageway that was wide enough to allow for the passage of horses, oxen, and the wagons they struggled to pull. It was less amazing, considering that nearly every road penetrated deeply into Indian territory, that Indian fighters were called upon to build those roads. At least one such road built by Indian fighters allowed an entire army to traverse the wilderness on its way to fight a battle.

To Build a Road

Eighteen-year-old Indian fighter James Smith heaved and sweated and swung his ax mightily, chopping down trees within the humid shade of the forest canopy. With each of his labored hacks, the mulched earth beneath his boots gave way under him. He could smell as well as feel the sun-starved, earthen dampness that was swallowing his feet. Smith and the dozen or so other young Virginians in his party had volunteered to cut a road through the wilderness for British general Edward Braddock's army of fifteen hundred men who were vaingloriously attempting to march four abreast through the trackless tangle with their flags, bright red uniforms, and banging wagons. Nothing but a deer path had marked this route before and, for his part, Smith was at least happy that the deer had shown them the few natural passes that existed through these towering Allegheny Mountains. Otherwise, he and the other Indian fighters would have had to carry out the time-consuming explorations required for blazing original trails from scratch.

So thanks to the migrating deer of eons past, they knew the quickest way to Fort Duquesne, where some three hundred hostile French soldiers and Indian braves were attempting to encroach on what they considered to be English land. What concerned them, more than their direction, though, were the growing number of Indian signs they were encountering along the way. A broken twig here, a moccasin print there, and a forest filled with animal sounds that everyone knew could well be the communications of a fierce and nearby enemy.

There was no way that they could mask the sound of their approach. Every chop of the ax echoed into three or four others and every man was generating twenty hacks a

Trailblazers in the East 33

British general Edward Braddock and his army march along a forest path forged by trailblazers. The trailblazers often had to stop and fight Indians along the way.

minute. With the tumbled-together whackings and splittings and cuttings and slammings, it sounded as if the forest was being assaulted by a flock of giant woodpeckers. And like all noise beneath the self-enclosed canopy, it reverberated for miles and in every direction, continuously exposing their position to anyone with ears to hear it.

But Smith and the others kept on working and chopping, heaving and cleaving, until their meaty arms burned with fatigue. And they pressed on through their fatigue and beyond. What else could they do but endure the blistered hands and sore feet and muscles that spasmed for want of salt. They were Indian fighters, albeit young ones, accustomed to hard work and unafraid of fighting. And if the Indians who lived nearby wanted to fight

over this trespass, they had already boasted, let them come and have it, which is exactly what the Indians did.

Where Has All the Bravado Gone?

"Pa-thack!", cracked a rifle, and then another and another. A woodcutter groaned and crumpled into the ferns. Smith plunged down beside him, terrified, clutching frantically at himself for signs of his own blood. He felt it; or was it urine? It did not matter. He would be dead soon, erasing all shame and fear. Clinging desperately to the damp earth, he saw his mother flash through his mind and cried out for her.

The air exploded with whooping, shrieking, soul-splitting horror. The Indians were charging through the brush, swinging their tomahawks over their heads. Shrilling guttural, ferocious cries, they pounced upon him, scattering all of his friends before he could even remember where his rifle was. But that did not matter either. He was suddenly surrounded and knew he would be dead soon. He waited, trembling, as the Indians conversed among themselves, and then he felt his head erupt into agonizing blackness, the victim of a tomahawk blow.

Young Smith awoke outside the sharpened-log palisade of Fort Duquesne with matted, bloody-black hair and a yawning, cavernous headache. Laughing Indians were shaking him back to consciousness, trilling cries that were just as curdling as before yet far louder and somehow more mocking. He shook his

Mother Flintlock

The weapon of choice for most eastern Indian fighters was the Kentucky or Pennsylvania long rifle. Its barrel differed from the common musket in an important way: the inside bore was cut with a spiraling groove called "rifling." The rifling spun or drilled the exiting bullet through the air straighter and farther than smoothbore muskets could, increasing the range of accuracy from fifty to three hundred yards.

Despite its advantages, a skilled rifleman could only load and fire his weapon once or perhaps twice a minute following a tedious sequence of steps that only practice and habit could begin to accelerate. These instructions show why.

To load a Kentucky flintlock rifle, the rifleman has to:

1. Take the powder horn (holding enough black powder for seventy-five shots) and fill the attached tiny measuring horn with the proper charge.
2. Pour the powder down the muzzle of the barrel and into the breech.
3. Reach back into the shooting bag (slung over one shoulder and hanging on the opposite hip) and take out a lead ball (bullet) and patch (cloth or leather).
4. Take the small patch knife hanging around the neck and cut the patch to fit around the ball.
5. Pull out the wooden ramrod from the slot beneath the barrel.
6. Place the patch-wrapped ball into the muzzle and ram it down into the breech with the ramrod.
7. Remove the ramrod and return it to the slot beneath the barrel.
8. Flip up the frizzen (the front of the flintlock mechanism, above the trigger), uncovering the small metal "flash pan."
9. Fill the pan with powder from the horn.
10. Flip back the frizzen.

At this point, the rifleman is ready to fire. He aims and pulls the trigger, causing the hammer to fall. The flint attached to the hammer strikes the steel of the flintlock's front flip-up piece and causes sparks to fly. The sparks ignite the powder in the pan, which sends fire down the gas vent into the breech. The larger charge there explodes, firing the lead ball out of the barrel. The rifleman waves away the cloud of white smoke, checks for damage done, and begins the reloading process all over again.

eyes clear and saw the source of the brain-piercing pandemonium. For a hundred yards or more, scores of the painted men stood in a human tunnel and jeered at him to come through. This was it, Smith knew, the gauntlet about which he had heard so many fearsome tales.

Torture, Execution, or Initiation?

Before he could react, the Indians nearest him threw him into it and hundreds of groping, grabbing arms began to tear at him. Each muscle-rippled arm swung a club or a rock or beat him with a fist. Every jack o'lantern face burned him with sardonic rage. They dragged him along, shrieking and assaulting, from one crazed sadist to the next. Over and over, the Indians pummeled and wracked him, crushed and blasted him, always pulling him to the next howling man.

Smith covered his head as best as he could but his battered arms could only protect him so much. He winced and grimaced and cried out in splintering pain with each of the thousand blows. He balled himself up like a pill bug but the Indians just shoved him through. Where was death, his shattered mind

The Necessaries

Pathfinding and Indian trading often went hand in hand. In an effort to establish trading relations with "undiscovered" Indians, Alexander Henry the Younger mapped out new routes throughout Canada and the United States. He traveled by foot, on horseback, and even on dog sled, amassing a personal fortune and blazing new trails. When provisioning a pathfinding expedition that would be partly undertaken by river, he made an entry in his journal, reprinted in Froncek's *Voices from the Wilderness*, that reflected what he considered to be essential for such a dual-purpose trip. Presumably, he and his men would dip into the trade goods when necessary.

Sunday, July 20th, 1800. The canoes have been given out to the men, to gum and prepare, I found everything ready for our departure; and early this morning gave out to all their respective loading, which consisted of 28 packages per canoe, namely:

Merchandise, 90 pounds each	5 bales
Canal Tobacco	1 bale
Kettles	1 bale
Guns	1 case
Iron works	1 case
New twist tobacco	2 rolls
Leaden balls	2 bags
Leaden shot	1 bag
Flour	1 bag
Sugar	1 keg
Gunpowder	2 kegs
High wine, 9 gallons each	10 kegs

Equipage for the voyage: Provisions for four men, 4 bags of corn, 1½ bushel in each; ½ keg grease; 4 packages of 90 pounds each private property belonging to the men consisting of clothing, tobacco, etc. for themselves so that when all hands were embarked, the canoes sunk to the gunnel.

Henry died by drowning in 1814, perhaps, one wonders, as a result of his canoe and himself being overloaded with "high wine."

Indians eye their white captives. Prisoners seldom survived the brutal Indian tortures.

pleaded. But it did not come and the beating went on although dark clouds began to crowd out the light. Flinching and hurting, he still stung with each blow, but soon he was drifting in and out of his razored suffering. He still heard the whoops, tasted blood, and spit a tooth out now and then, but at last Smith let his tenacity go and he slipped into a dreamless oblivion so deep that even the pain could not follow. But his ordeal was not yet over.

From Witness to Warrior

"The next thing I remember," he later wrote,

> was a French doctor standing over me, who had opened a vein in my left arm. I told him I felt much pain but was able to walk. About sun down I beheld a small party coming into the fort with about a dozen more prisoners, stripped naked, with their hands tied behind their backs,

and their faces and part of their bodies blacked—these prisoners they burned to death. I stood until I beheld them begin to burn one of these men, they had him tied to a stake and kept touching him with fire-brands and red-hot irons and he screamed in a most doleful manner—the Indians in the mean time yelling like infernal spirits. As this scene appeared too shocking for me to behold, I retired to my lodging both sore and sorry, convinced that I would be burned next and all for building a road for a defeated army that would never go through.[13]

Braddock's Road, renamed Forbes' Road, did eventually go through, but not in 1755, and not because of the efforts of James Smith and his young Indian fighters. And for reasons he never understood, the Indians never burned him alive like the others. Instead, they initiated him into their tribe, and this onetime fighter of Indians began a five-year odyssey of being an Indian, learning their ways, and becoming an expert in their methods of forest guerrilla warfare. When he escaped, he took his knowledge and skills and plied them ruthlessly as one of the frontier's most feared Indian fighters. And he never lost his appreciation for any road he ever traveled through Indian lands.

The Road into Kentucky

During the mid-1770s, Daniel Boone achieved his first measure of fame as a trailblazer. He blazed a trail through the eastern mountains and into the forested flatlands of Kentucky on the other side. With thirty other ax-wielding Indian fighters, he widened an ancient Indian trail, the Warrior's Path, to accommodate a single-file pack train of horses and thereby linked North Carolina with "Kain-tuck-ee" and the distant Ohio River. Boone had been along this path previously as a solitary "longhunter" but this was the first time he had chopped down or notched enough trees to show others the way. He later widened the trail into a road, the Wilderness Road, with room enough for wagons so that he could guide his and other families to their new home of Boonesborough.

Said one biographer in the 1840s, "It was not Boone's nature to be long at rest. There were still boundless tracts of rich lands to be explored, so, shouldering his rifle, he once more bade adieu to civilization, and plunged alone into the wilderness, to open new roads for the tide of emigration that was soon to follow."[14]

Along with the boldest settlers, the first few waves of that tide included substantial numbers of Indian fighters, hunters, and trappers, most of whom had been enculturated to consider the Indians as vermin more safely exterminated than reasoned with. Unfortunately for the Indians, they were the first to establish regular contact and very often conflict with the natives of Kentucky. And they felt no qualms about killing them and taking their land. Even the threat of punishment at the hands of the white man's legal system did not preclude these first Indian fighters from attempting to wipe out any and all Indians they encountered and they were not going to wait for the army to do it "legally." One defiant Indian fighter said in 1783, "The people of Kentucky will carry on private expeditions against the Indians and kill them whenever they meet them, and I do not believe that there is a jury in all Kentucky who would pun-

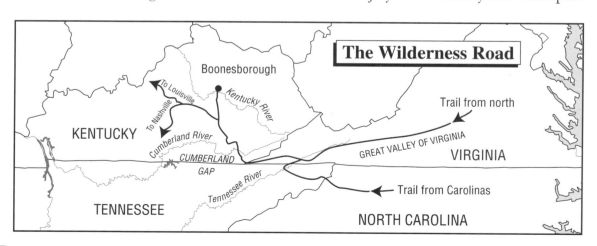

John Filson, who appended the "autobiography" of Daniel Boone to his *Discovery, Settlement, and Present State of Kentucke* in 1784, undoubtedly put flowery words into the mouth of the undereducated trailblazer. However, the essence of what he had Boone say accurately reflected the man's abiding awe, respect, and sensitivity for the wonders of nature that he, as the first white witness, experienced upon seeing it. According to Filson, Boone recalled his initial pathfinding venture into the Kentucky wilderness not with a conquering spirit but rather with an almost childlike appreciation.

It was the first of May, in the year 1769, that I resigned my domestic happiness for a time, and left my family and peaceable habitation on the Yadkin River, in North Carolina, to wander through the wilderness of America in quest of the country of Kentucky, in company with John Finlay, John Stewart, Joseph Holden, James Monay, and William Cool. We proceeded successfully, and after a long and fatiguing journey through a mountainous wilderness, in a westward direction, on the seventh day of June following, we found ourselves on Red River and, from the top of an eminence, saw with pleasure the beautiful level of Kentucky.

On one pleasing ramble, we passed through a great forest on which stood myriads of trees, some gay with blossoms, others with fruits. Nature here was a series of wonders, and a fund of delight; here she displayed her ingenuity and industry in a variety of flowers and fruits, beautifully colored, elegantly shaped, and charmingly flavored; and we were diverted by grand and innumerable animals presenting themselves perpetually to our view.

Clearly, the heart of at least one Indian fighter was more complex and tender than the tales of bloody battles alone might lead us to presume.

ish a man for it." [15] And the sentiment was the same to the north and the south.

Blazing Trails Through Tennessee and Ohio

At about the same time, Tennessee opened up due to the prodigious ax-work of woodsmen and Indian fighters under James Robertson and John Sevier, who also notched trees on either side of the proposed route and cut them entirely down when necessary to indicate the way for subsequent settlers. The small party of hearty trailblazers skirmished with Indians and swung their hatchets until their road, the Old Walton Road, stretched from South Carolina to the present site of Nashville.

In 1797 an Indian fighter by the name of Ebenezer Zane accepted a promise of land from the government of the United States to clear a path through the eastern Ohio wilderness that would connect Wheeling, Virginia (now West Virginia) with Maysville, Kentucky, the jump-on point for the trail to New Orleans. This blazed trail, or trace, became known as Zane's Trace and eventually opened the riches of the South and West to American northerners. Somewhat atypically, an Ohio

Men load a pack mule as it patiently withstands their tugging to secure the bulky load.

historian notes, this particular trailblazer was well remunerated for his services. "For his work in opening the Trace, Zane was granted by Congress the right to locate his military land parcel where the Trace crossed the three main rivers (around present-day Zanesville, Ohio) and, owning such an important cross-roads, he went on to a life of prominence."[16]

Packing the Trailblazers' Goods

A well-executed trailblazing expedition required careful preparations. Only the most rational and far-sighted frontiersmen ever returned from a pathfinding trip whose course and destination were as dangerous and unknown to them as Christopher Columbus's had been three hundred years earlier or a manned space probe is to modern explorers. Consequently, most trailblazers gathered together as many healthy horses and mules as practicable, sometimes as many as four or five per man. Even if the men had to walk themselves due to a narrow path or no path at all,

the amount of gear that they had to pack in with them could only be borne on the backs of four-legged beasts of burden.

The trailblazers' pack trains might include from a dozen to a hundred horses and mules. Most blazers preferred horses, smaller and more nimble ones at that instead of bulky, muscular horses capable of carrying more cargo. The clumsier, more durable mules had the strongest backs of all, but their legendary stubbornness often kept pathfinders from taking them along. They usually required so much loud profanity to get and keep them moving that it was impossible to proceed through uncharted Indian country without being detected.

The master driver rode the first horse and, behind him, each horse's lead rein was tied to the split, wooden packsaddle of the animal it followed. The train proceeded in single file with men riding at intervals to keep the baggage and the horses in order. The master driver's assistant brought up the rear, ready to solve all problems with the horses and cargo as they might arise. But each man in the party was responsible for keeping all the goods securely cinched to all of the pack-saddles.

The packsaddles of well-organized trail-blazing expeditions contained everything that the animals might conceivably need while traveling in an unknown land perhaps devoid of resources. As staples, the horses carried their own feed, usually a mix of corn, peas, and beans. Wild grazing grasses and clovers would suffice when available, but no sensible frontiersman would count on finding vegetation at all times. At night, the men used strips of rawhide to hobble the horses, tying their back legs together so they could not run off. If there

was a reasonable assurance that Indians were not in the area, they would also dig out cowbells to tie around the horses' necks, in order to locate by sound any animals that might manage to stray in spite of their hobbled legs.

Dried Meat for the Long Haul

Even in the animal-rich eastern woodlands, pack animals sometimes became meals for the men if they ran out of gunpowder. The possibility that they might have to eat their animals provided another reason for pathfinders to graze their horses and mules to the point of fattening before delving too deeply into the wilderness. The more organized expedition leaders had their men hunt and process the meat into jerky before they left. Deer, the meat of which is called venison, was usually the food of choice for the eastern men.

Historian Edward Tunis comments on diet on the trail: "These people knew how to preserve meat by soaking it in brine; the difficulty was to get enough salt for the purpose. Meat was also heavily smoked, without salt, to preserve it. They cured most of their meat by cutting it into strips and drying it before a fire into what they called jerky, or jerk. They dried squash, too, as the Indians did."[17] Food preserved that way could serve as rations whenever fresh game could not be found and could conveniently be eaten without any additional cooking any time wet weather or the proximity of hostile Indians precluded the building of fires.

An Indian scout points out a trail to the master driver. Such scouts had expert knowledge of the wilderness.

Cornmeal: An Indian Gift

No expedition attempted to penetrate the wilderness without bags upon bags of corn-meal, the staple Indians undoubtedly wished

Portrait of a Trailblazer

Eastern dime novelists, newspapermen, and magazine editors were always on the prowl for actual frontier events that they could exploit and inflate into escapades of superhuman courage in order to sell their "rags" to a gullible public. What resulted was a steady stream of hogwash about pathfinders single-handedly capturing entire tribes of Indians, shooting the eyes out of bears from distances of several miles, and dressing like top-hatted and formally attired dandies while fighting the currents of frothing rivers in their canoes. One Indian fighter tried to set the record straight, at least regarding his appearance, by describing what he commonly looked like in the wild. His account (in the third person) appears in Robert Cleland's *This Reckless Breed of Men:*

A trapper sports the buckskin, long hair, and beard of a man far from civilization.

His skin, from constant exposure, assumes a hue almost as dark as the aborigine, and his features and physical structure attain a rough and hardy cast. His hair, through inattention, becomes long, coarse, and bushy, and loosely dangles upon his shoulders. His head is surmounted by a low crowned wool hat, or a rude substitute of his own manufacture. His clothes are of buckskin, gaily fringed at the seams with strings of the same material, cut and made in a fashion peculiar to himself and his associates. The deer and buffalo furnish him the required covering for his feet. . . . His waist is encircled by a belt of leather, holding encased his butcher-knife and pistols—while from his neck is suspended a bullet-pouch securely fastened to the belt in front, and beneath the right arm hangs a powder-horn traversely from his shoulder, behind which, upon the strap attached to it, are affixed his bullet-mould, ball-screw, wiper, awl, etc. With a gun-ramming stick made of some hard wood and a good rifle placed in his hands, carrying from thirty-five balls to the pound, the reader will have before him a correct likeness of a genuine mountaineer when fully equipped.

Add to this image the stench of sweat, oils, dirt, human waste, animal guts, blood, sulfurous gunpowder, and every other body odor made rancid by constant work and infrequent bathing, and the likeness of the mountaineer tends to become more vivid; though taking a form that few eastern writers would have wanted to include in their books for "civilized" readers.

Deer provided most of the meat for the men in the wilderness. Only when gunpowder was in short supply were the animals difficult to hunt.

they had never shared with the white man. The original kernel corn was ground into dust between two circular stones about two feet across turned in a box by two men (or, within the confines of settlement walls, by boys). Once on the trail there were various ways in which to cook the meal, all of which methods had been assimilated from the Indians. They made hominy by soaking the hard kernels with small amounts of lye to soften and loosen the hard outer shells and then washing the mush thoroughly with water to remove the husks. The hominy softened and swelled and became snowy white when it was boiled into a mush that could be sweetened with honey or maple syrup. Tunis further explains:

> Johnnycake and corn pone were for breakfast and midday dinner, in that order. Both were made as quite thin batters with water, soda, and salt. Johnnycake [or journey cake] thereby became quite dry so that it would keep as the ration for the traveler. . . . The skillet made a good pan for cooking johnnycake slowly, next to the fire but not over it. If a pan was lacking a flat stone would serve. The finished article was crisp and not much more than half an inch thick. The same batter could be thinned and fried in the skillet as "can dodgers."[18]

Other Culinary Delights

Besides the favored deer and buffalo, the trailblazers hunted bear, wild turkey, and elk. They even ate any panthers they had to kill in self-defense, remarking that they tasted much like veal or rattlesnake. As secondary fare they ate porcupine, beaver, and opossum but they preferred the meat of squirrels when they could kill enough of them to make a proper stew. They avoided destroying their tiny bodies during the hunt by "barking" them, shooting the tree just beside the squirrels' heads and killing the little creatures by concussion alone.

Depending on the time of year, trailblazers might be able to bring migrating duck, goose, and swan to the dinner fire. Pigeons also promised a tasty meal as they flew overhead in sky-blackening flocks. And last but certainly not least was the corn liquor that served as a carefully rationed staple at every meal. Room was always set aside on a horse

Just What the Doctor Ordered

Trailblazers had to be prepared for every possible emergency, including but not limited to hostile Indians, natural disasters, wild animals, and acts of God. However, no amount of preparation against these perils did them much good if they became sick or injured on their journey. To treat such physical maladies, pathfinders could rely on only a few remedies, as the state of medicine during the eighteenth and early nineteenth centuries was little more advanced than it had been in the Dark Ages.

This is not to imply that the trailblazers' medicine could do no good. In fact, some of their remedies were later developed into the scientifically proven treatments of the modern era. For example, foxglove leaves, which prevented many frontier heart attacks, became the basis for the contemporary cardiac stimulus digitalis. Bark from the cinchona family of trees could cure high fevers as its derivative, quinine, does today; and the active ingredient in the juice that the pathfinders squeezed from the belladonna plant to relieve abdominal cramps relieves muscle spasms in its modern form, atropine.

Mineral springs containing the standard modern treatment for manic depression, lithium carbonate, raised and calmed spirits as effectively then as now, and the jack-in-the-pulpit plant, used on the frontier to effectively treat the symptoms of colds and pneumonia, is still the basis of medications treating the same ailments. Bathing wounds in saltwater reduced swelling and promoted healing just as saline solutions can in our own age. Pathfinders also knew the danger of infections and successfully fought them the only way they could: by burning them out with gunpowder or boiling oil.

Perhaps the state of frontier medicine is best summed up, however, by an Indian fighter who had spent a great portion of his life trailblazing roads for others to follow. As quoted in Richard Dunlop's *Doctors of the American Frontier*, he said simply, "Before proper doctors, medical treatment was largely a matter of whiskey, a hunting knife, and nature; knocking a man out with the whiskey, probing for the bullet or arrowhead with the knife, and putting on a plaster of some kind of plant afterwards. We dressed them and God cured them."

to pack a keg into the hinterland to quench the thirsts, anxieties, and passions of men who risked death every day to make a living. The golden elixir further served as a prized trade item when negotiating with the eastern Indians.

Western trailblazers tried to pack even more of the intoxicant than their brothers back East since they had much more land and many more Indians with whom to deal than those in Kentucky, Ohio, Pennsylvania, and Tennessee. In fact, whiskey nearly took on greater importance in the Rocky Mountains as a medicine than as an inebriant, for the trails through them proved even more bloody to blaze than those through the Appalachians.

Pathfinding West of the Mississippi

The dense forests of the East gave way to plains and deserts west of the Mississippi River. Even the pine stands on western slopes were less thicketed beneath their boughs and more easily traveled. Indian fighters establishing trails in the West, however, had to spend more time finding passes through snow-capped peaks and linking water holes in the arid country. But, the western Indian fighters with their "cousins" in the East had one significant challenge in common: Both groups found a peaceful, gift-bearing approach worked best at times and fighting became unavoidable at others. In one important incident, a blustery but successful bluff allowed for the ultimate success of the greatest pathfinding expedition in American history.

A Tense Beginning

A mounted party of Indians, Teton Sioux, appeared on the bank of the upper Missouri River in September of 1804 and indicated through signs that their chiefs desired a meeting with the "chiefs" of the strange sailed boat trespassing up their river. Meriwether Lewis and William Clark, leading a party of some fifty soldiers and Indian fighters, accepted the offer and allowed several Sioux leaders to board their fifty-five-foot keelboat. Soon after, the number of braves armed with bows and arrows increased on the shoreline as if to offer a show of force. In full dress uniform and tricornered hat, Captain William Clark led eighteen of their men ashore with an

Lewis, Clark (center), and their men listen attentively to the instructions of Sacagewea, their Indian guide.

intimidating display of their own. "They were not afraid of any Indians," Lewis would write of the landing party, "and they would open fire with their muskets if necessary."[19] Clearly, both sides were preparing for a showdown.

The talks on the keelboat began amicably enough but quickly soured. Lewis wrote, "The chiefs were exceedingly fond of the whiskey offered them. They took up the empty bottle, smelled it, and made many excited gestures for more, and became troublesome when they did not get it."[20] It soon became apparent that neither side had translators capable of resolving the escalating situation diplomatically, so Lewis ordered the chiefs forcibly removed from the keelboat.

Sometimes the Indian fighter's most important skill was not killing Indians but making peace with them. In an effort to jointly calm, frighten, and impress the roiling Indians on shore, Captain Clark resorted to a display of his soldiers' precision marching and drilling ability. He further demonstrated a newfangled air rifle to which he attempted to attribute vague magical and spiritual powers and he burned up a few leaves with a magnifying glass. To add a bit of sweetening to the display, he offered them medallions, flags, tobacco twists, and army coats and hats. But that was obviously not going to be good enough, for one of the Sioux chiefs ordered one of the smaller boats to be seized and then blurted out the Indians' first direct threat. Clark wrote of him, "He was very insolent in both words and gestures. He pretended drunkenness and staggered up against us, declaring that we could not go on, stating that he had not received presents sufficient from us. His gestures were of such a personal na-

Lewis and Clark tried to avoid conflict with the Indians. Here, they try to forge an agreement with a group of Indians that will let them explore the tribe's land without harassment.

The Way to an Indian's Heart

When commissioning Meriwether Lewis and William Clark to lead what he called the U.S. Corps of Discovery, President Thomas Jefferson specifically ordered them to avoid conflicts with the natives if at all possible. Due to equal parts of bravery, bluff, and seemingly innate skills in diplomacy, Lewis and Clark lost none of their men to Indian hostilities and killed two Native Americans during the entire two-and-a-half years in the wilderness. For fifty hardened Indian fighters, that demonstrated both their great restraint and the power of the bead. In his *Journals*, Meriwether Lewis wrote:

> The objects of foreign trade which are most desired are the common cheap, blue or white beads of about fifty or seventy to the penny weight which are strung on strands a fathom in length and sold by the yard or the length of both arms. Of these, blue beads, which are called tia commachuck, or chief beads, hold the first rank in their ideas of relative value. The most inferior kind are es-

teemed beyond the finest wampum and are temptations which can always seduce them to part with their most valuable effects. Indeed, if the example of civilized life did not completely vindicate their choice, we might wonder at their infatuated attachment to a bauble in itself so worthless. Yet these beads are, perhaps, quite as reasonable objects of research as the precious metals since they are at once beautiful ornaments for the person and the great calculating medium of trade with all the nations on the rivers.

And in the end, the Native Americans' dependency on the commerce and economy of the white man that began with the sparkling little beads probably did more to defeat the many tribes than did the Indian fighters' bullets and blades. Prudent Indian fighters usually tried that approach first anyway, falling back on violence only when they had to. Which, unfortunately, tended to be often.

---

ture I felt myself compelled to draw my sword and make a signal to the boat to prepare for action."[21]

To the Brink of Battle

Thus, the first showdown ensued between the United States and the feared nation of the Sioux. Some seventy-five Indians knocked arrows into their bowstrings as fewer than twenty soldiers and Indian fighters rattled their single-shot muskets to the ready. A few Sioux even produced antique shotguns (probably provided by earlier

French or English traders) and the frontiersmen onboard the keelboat quickly loaded their swivel cannons and blunderbusses. Nerves crackled, stomachs tightened yet neither side showed any sign of flinching. Veteran Indian fighter William Clark puffed out his chest, grit his teeth, and stared down the chiefs before him. Onboard the keelboat, Lewis ordered his thirty-odd men to battle stations. Every man swallowed hard and took aim at a target, knowing that in the next few wildly thumping heartbeats, he could very easily die.

To prove the bravery, power, and "medicine" of the white man, Clark ordered his

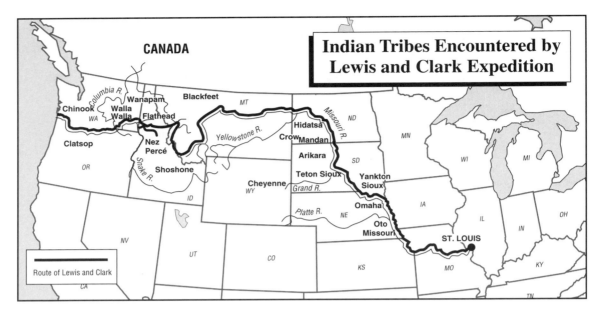

Indian Tribes Encountered by Lewis and Clark Expedition

CANADA

Chinook · Walla Walla · Wanapam · Blackfeet · Flathead · Clatsop · Nez Percé · Shoshone · Hidatsa · Crow · Mandan · Arikara · Cheyenne · Teton Sioux · Yankton Sioux · Omaha · Oto · Missouri

Columbia R. · Yellowstone R. · Snake R. · Missouri R. · Grand R. · Platte R.

ST. LOUIS

WA · OR · NV · CA · ID · UT · MT · WY · CO · ND · SD · NE · KS · MN · IA · MO · WI · IL · MI · IN · OH · KY · TN

Route of Lewis and Clark

soldiers onshore to row back out to the boat, whereupon he turned, erect, tall, and proud. Standing alone, he pierced the eyes and souls of every Indian facing him, bracing to meet death yet utterly convinced that his solitary posturing was all that could possibly prevent a fight. Brandishing his saber, Clark boldly bluffed that he had "more medicine on board his boat than could kill twenty such nations as the Sioux in one day," that the expedition "must and would go on," and that he and his men "were not squaws but warriors."[22] Then he performed a precise about-face and strode defiantly away, belittling the Indians by not even glancing back.

His fearlessness, more feigned than felt, stunned the Sioux and planted doubt in their minds as to whether they should or even could harm these courageous and mysterious strangers. Perhaps they did possess some unknown and powerful medicine. When a party of Indian fighters landed and fanned out, the Sioux began to waver. Soon, they were fading to the rear clearly the first to blink in this monumental stare-down.

Thus this small party, everyone a skilled trailblazer, explorer, and adventurer, proceeded up river into the dangerous unknown reaches of what would become, thanks in great part to their efforts, the northern and northwestern United States, one-third of the eventual American landmass, comprising ten large states. The pathways they discovered and mapped there were destined to not only serve as the first water route connecting the eastern United States to the Pacific Ocean but spin off endless miles of other river routes and trails that would eventually interconnect the entire West.

The Fruits of Diplomacy

The trails blazed by Lewis and Clark not only pointed the direction for thousands of travelers to "the Great Western Sea" but spawned many other benefits as well. They opened the way for Americans to settle the Oregon Territory, securing the young nation's claim to it while other claimants without their settlers there, such as England, Russia, and Spain, lost interest in the "Americanizing" region. And while many nations of Indians that the expedition's pathfinders "discovered" did go to war with the United States later, the trailblazing Indian fighters laid the groundwork for better relations with countless other tribes. Also, the potential natural resources the white men discovered shifted the sights and energies of more and more American businessmen from the Atlantic seaboard to the wide-open West.

All those benefits would have been lost, however, or at least delayed for a critical time, if the guns and arrows had fired that day on the banks of the muddy Missouri River. If nerves had snapped and trigger fingers jerked, many Sioux and nearly all of the Indian fighters would have died. The trails discovered and the knowledge they gleaned would have remained in the realm of mythology until another party of rare and gifted frontiersmen was gathered. And their success would not have been guaranteed had they not possessed that most necessary of all Indian fighting talents: peacemaking. For in the end, surviving the daily life of the Indian fighter meant figuring out ways to fight as few Indians as possible.

More Diplomacy and Another Path Found

At about the time Lewis and Clark were conducting their expedition, a young, handsome, and overly ambitious army lieutenant named Zebulon Pike led a party of twenty soldiers and Indian fighters north from St. Louis along the Mississippi River with orders to locate that river's source. On the way he was to establish diplomatic and economic relations with the various tribes he encountered in hopes of wooing their allegiances and fur

trading business from the British. This part of the assignment would require great restraint for this combative lieutenant, who had for several years been trying to make a name for himself by killing as many Indians as possible east of the Mississippi.

Preparation for the trip, however, came easily for Pike, who had served previously as a supply officer at a frontier army post. With only two thousand dollars, he procured enough flour, salt, cornmeal, pork, whiskey, lead, paper, ink, warm clothing, and blankets to last twenty robust men on a four-month keelboat journey. To aid in the collection of scientific information, Pike took along a thermometer, a watch, and a device to navigate by the stars. Perhaps most importantly, he brought gifts for the Indians he would be meeting: knives, trinkets, beads, American flags, bright cloth, and of course, plenty of whiskey. Any other food the party needed, the hunters would provide, he assumed. Plentiful

Army lieutenant Zebulon Pike led an expedition to discover the source of the Mississippi River.

herds of elk, deer, and buffalo would be roaming freely, at least until the deep snows fell. And he would have the men back in St. Louis by then. Or so he said.

Though well supplied, interminable hours poling the seventy-foot keelboat upstream soon had every crewman griping, grousing, and grumbling. They could not wait for the first impassable rapids to appear so that they could build canoes or buy them from some Indians. Their grousing did not end, even when they made the switch to canoes, however. For one thing, twelve hours of paddling the smaller vessels left them just as fatigued as had slaving on the keelboat. For another, the Minnesota winter was beginning to set in and they discovered their imperious leader had either lied or blundered. He had packed only one tent, his own. All the other men had to huddle together, shivering in the open around fires too weak to do them any good. It soon became clear they were not going to be able to accomplish their mission and make it home before the bitterest of snows fell. And fall they did, by the foot and yard, until the frozen river forced the men from their canoes into hastily constructed wooden sleds that they had to pull like mush dogs.

The Painful Truth

Pike kept up his journal when his ink did not freeze. In one entry written from his tent, he wrote, "Most days the party is able to make only a few miles . . . never did I undergo more fatigue. Some of the men have had their noses . . . fingers, and . . . toes frozen."[23] In that era, when frozen toes and fingers turned white, then black with stinking rot, they usually had to be amputated with little more than whiskey, a sharp ax, and four strong men to hold the patient down. Yet Pike drove the

party on for five months longer than the original plan called for—until they had accomplished their mission.

More Trails and More Disappointment

Pike returned to St. Louis convinced that his place in history had been secured. After all, he had made peace with the northern Indians and even convinced the Santee Sioux to sell the crucial area of Minnesota on which Minneapolis and St. Paul stand today and which served shortly afterward as the site of one of the frontier's most important forts. He had confronted and discouraged the British fur traders from doing business in the area and encouraged the Indians to begin shifting their trade to the Americans. All in all, Pike had every reason to be proud of himself and to expect a hero's reception throughout the country for himself and his Indian fighters.

He did not get it, however, because Lewis and Clark arrived back in St. Louis a little ahead of the Pike expedition and "stole" all the glory that was "rightfully" his. Embittered, he fell in with another group of army officers dissatisfied with their slow rise to fame. He accepted their offer to blaze a trail into the unknown region to the west. Along the way, he would discover Pike's Peak in Colorado, scout the southwestern lands of Spanish Mexico to the south, and suffer the spreading fame of Lewis and Clark and the new Indian fighters they spawned.

A Path Found Through "Colter's Hell"

On Lewis and Clark's return trip, one of their finest Indian fighters asked to be freed of his

An 1890 photograph captures the grandeur of Yellowstone Valley. John Colter was the first white to explore the unusual area, filled with geothermal wonders.

commitment to the expedition. John Colter (who later ran naked to escape the Indians) had received an offer to trap furs in areas that even Lewis and Clark had not explored. To Colter, the lure must have been overwhelming: to experience lands that no white man had ever experienced and possibly to make a fortune trapping an as-yet-untapped supply of beaver.

Setting off on his own with nothing more in mind than to find a few Indian tribes with which to trade his pelts, Colter embarked on a trek of hundreds of trackless miles through the Montana and Wyoming mountains, across the Continental Divide, fording and refording endless streams and rivers until he found himself in a natural wonderland that not even he could fathom; a geographical melange of

hot springs, boiling mud holes, and geysers. He knew that William Clark had remarked of this area from a distance, "There is frequently a loud noise like thunder, which makes the earth tremble. Indians state that they seldom go there because their children cannot sleep and conceive it possessed of spirits who were adverse that men should be near them."[24]

For his part, Colter later said that "a fellow can catch a fish in an icy river there, pull it into a boiling pool, and cook his fish without ever having to take it off the hook."[25] He used Shoshone Indian mythology to explain its formation: "A medicine man cursed the whole region and turned the trees to stone."[26] Until the trail Colter blazed through this cauldron of blasting fountains and scalding mud pointed the way for the entire world to see it, no

Lieutenant Zebulon Pike's name has acquired much of the fame he so earnestly sought while alive but never received. Pike's Peak, which he discovered but neither climbed nor named, made him nationally famous, but not until pioneers in their wagon trains began using it as a landmark many years after Pike's death.

Opportunity for more lasting fame, or infamy, may yet come as historians unearth more letters and official documents suggesting that he took part in a conspiracy to break the western states and territories away from the infant United States. Aaron Burr, former vice president and the victor in his duel with Alexander Hamilton, appears to have led this nefarious quest with the help of one General James Wilkinson in order to form their own country. Pike has been implicated by association if nothing else because Wilkinson had long been his sponsor and confidant, and Pike was the "son Wilkinson never had."

Wilkinson needed espionage information on the Spanish army then occupying Mexico, California, and the Southwest. He and Burr knew that they would have to fight the Spanish as well as the Americans if they were to successfully set up their own breakaway empire in the West. And who could be better suited for such an undertaking than Wilkinson's own "son," Zebulon Pike.

So it appears to have been with these shaded motives that Pike blazed the first trail across what he called the Great Western desert, traded with the Indians along the way, and got himself arrested by the Spanish army, which just happened to enable him to learn its troop distribution, strength, and skill level. This was all priceless information to the conspirators whose new country would be bordering Spanish Mexico and Pike's sponsors considered his observations highly informative in all regards.

The fact that the Burr conspiracy was discovered and quashed before it could take root enabled Zebulon Pike's possible involvement to go unnoticed. The irony is rich, however, when considering that his recently discovered seditious activities may earn him the fame and attention that his truly remarkable pathfinding expeditions never did.

one then believed the full extent of his "tall tales." It would take government expeditions launched into "Colter's Hell" many years later to substantiate his reports and give it its ultimate name, Yellowstone National Park.

Stumbling into California

Jedediah Smith was one of the stoutest, most fearless Indian fighters west of the Mississippi River, and he fancied himself as a shrewd businessman as well. He set off in 1826 to blaze a new trail to suspected "beaver waters" southwest of Utah, and at first it looked like he might find them. The hills started out green and the rivers were wide, but the prairie grass soon gave way to sand. Jed Smith and his fifteen other Indian fighters had entered into the unforgiving Mojave Desert, the first white Americans to do so.

With enormous endurance and a talent for staying alive, they drove on into withering heat and eye-stinging sandstorms. What had begun as a trapping trip and then a pathfinding expedition was now simply a quest to survive. By accident, they found a route, however dangerous, from the Rocky Mountains to southern California, but these sun-blistered and desert-parched men cared little about that just then. All they wanted, they needed, they had to have to live were food and water. Smith later wrote:

> There for many days we had traveled weary, hungry, and thirsty drinking from springs that would only increase our thirst and looking in vain for a boundary of the interminable waste of sands. We had lost so many horses that we were all on foot—my men and the remainder of the horses were worn out with fatigue and hardships and emaciated with hunger. This was truly a country of starvation.[27]

But it was also a country through which thousands would now follow, though better supplied with food and water, to reach the fabled lands of California.

A Black Man in a Red World

The son of a Virginia slave girl and her white overseer punched one of the first trails through the snowy Sierra Nevadas and into northern California in search of new "beaver waters." That, however, seems to have been one of the least colorful of Jim Beckwourth's many exploits. Through bluff and bravery, he worked himself into the role of chief among the Crow Indians. He lied to an aged chieftain and his wife that he was their long-lost infant son returned to them at last and entitled to leadership in the tribe. The old "parents" might have doubted him at first but decided that someone as courageous and outrageous as this blustering young man must certainly be their son; at that, the entire village "nearly

welcomed me to death."[28] Or so Beckwourth boasted later.

His prowess as a lover may have surpassed his Indian fighting skills. He claimed to have married upwards of twelve wives while living with the Crow and another two with the Blackfeet, the Crows' most hated enemies. Of his experiences with the Blackfeet, Beckwourth wrote, "I soon rose to be a great man among them. One of the chiefs offered me his daughter for a wife. But there was a slight difficulty in my family affairs." That "slight difficulty" was his hatcheting, nearly to death, of his bride when she disobeyed him regarding an inconsequential matter. As he happily put it, "I dropped her as if a ball had pierced her heart."[29] He

Jim Beckwourth, the Indian fighter who became a chief of the Crow Indians.

eventually left the Blackfeet but not before his father-in-law, his near-dead wife's father, forgave him unconditionally for the assault. The chief took advantage of the opportunity to espouse to all the men in the tribe, "That thing disobeyed her husband. When your wives disobey your commands, you kill them; that is your right." [30]

An Indian-Loving Indian Fighter

Jim Bridger would have disagreed, for he took just one Indian wife and cherished her for a lifetime. But upon other issues such as morality, religion, family, and customs, this lean six-footer "made mostly of rawhide" agreed with the Indians wholeheartedly. When he was not living with them, he was trapping, fighting en-

Scout and trapper Jim Bridger claimed to be the first white to discover the Great Salt Lake.

emy Indians, and exploring and trailblazing paths all over the West: paths first for trappers and then for soldiers, Pony Express riders, farmers, and ranchers.

In terms of his trailblazing legacy, perhaps his discovery of the Great Salt Lake had the most impact, opening the way for overland travel into what is now Utah and, eventually, leading the Mormons there. Taking a bet that he and his horse could not traverse the perilous trails and cliffs through which the thunderous Bear River charged, young Jim Bridger set out alone in 1824 and disappeared for more than two weeks.

A man who interviewed Bridger later said that, during this time,

> He went where the river passes through the mountains and there he discovered the Great Salt Lake. He went to the margin and tasted the icy water and, on his return, reported his discovery. The salty taste of the water induced him, at first, to believe that this was an inland arm of the Pacific Ocean but, regardless of what he may have initially thought, Jim Bridger was the first discoverer of the Great Salt Lake. [31]

No record exists as to whether or not the bet was paid but the record is clear that, in time, the entire continent took note of his strange discovery.

Taking to the whitewater to test a possible shortcut on the Bighorn River, Bridger single-handedly rocketed a driftwood raft down what the Indians had long called "Bad Pass," a steep canyon of the Bighorn River that no man, white or Indian, had ever risked descending. A writer who knew Bridger, related the Indian fighter's impressions of the adventure: "The river's passage through this chain was rough and violent; making repeated falls, and rushing down long and furious rapids,

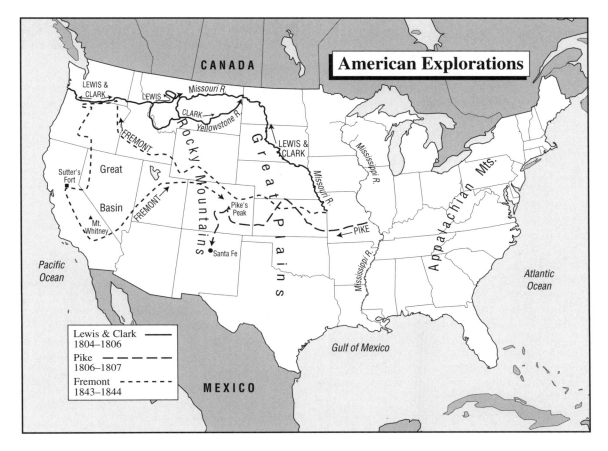

American Explorations

Lewis & Clark
1804–1806

Pike
1806–1807

Fremont
1843–1844

which threatened destruction to the navigator."[32] Nevertheless, Jim Bridger blasted down the virgin rapids on his raft piercing hidden reaches and finding paths that were theretofore unknown.

Later on, he built Fort Bridger in Wyoming, where the Oregon Trail split southwestward to California. Even though he did not personally lead many parties down the trail, he was always happy to draw maps of the routes he had helped to open up. One emigrant remarked of Bridger, "He was excessively kind and patient with me in laying down the route to Salt Lake, taking the trouble of drawing a chart with charcoal on the door, pointing out a new line that no one but he had attempted, which would be a shortcut

of thirty miles."[33] Had Jim Bridger had the political connections and social status of "the Great Pathfinder" himself, Captain John C. Fremont, he and not Fremont would have ended up as the most famous of all the western trailblazers.

The Pathfinder and His Friend

Without doubt, the best-known explorer and trailblazer in his own time was John C. Fremont. His reputation rested mostly on the facts that he was blatantly ambitious and a skilled social climber and had a devoted wife (the daughter of Thomas Hart Benton, a prominent U.S. senator from Missouri) who

The Greatest Trailblazer that History Forgot

Daniel Boone, Lewis and Clark, Jim Bridger, John C. Fremont, and Kit Carson are all names that evoke an immediate image: the rugged frontiersman, the opener of new lands, the Indian-fighting trailblazer who led America to its Manifest Destiny. But what about Joe Walker? Shouldn't he be remembered, too? Daniel Conner's biography, *Joseph Reddeford Walker*, examines this little-known pathfinder.

Said one who knew him, "Mr. Walker was a man well-calculated to under take pathfinding. He was well-hardened to the hardships of the wilderness—understood the character of the Indians very well—was kind and affable to his men, but at the same time at liberty to command without giving offense—and to explore unknown regions was his chief delight."

Although he and his parties broke new ground in every corner of the West, his most significant discoveries were those he made crossing the Sierra Nevadas into California. An Indian fighter who accompanied him wrote:

> We were at a complete standstill. No one was acquainted with the country, nor no person knew how wide the summit of this mountain was. We had traveled for five days since we arrived at what we supposed to be the summit—were now still surrounded by snow and jagged peaks. Finally, we reached the crest and here we began to encounter in our path many small streams which would shoot out from under these high snowbanks, and after running a short distance in deep chasms which they have through the ages cut in the rocks, precipitate themselves from one lofty precipice to another, until they are exhausted in rain below. Some of these precipices appeared to us to be more than a mile high.

Joe Walker and his men thus became the first white men to view the biblical grandeur of the Yosemite Valley. Many of them would claim until their dying day that that moment was the most exhilarating of their lives. Walker himself paid the experience the highest tribute he could: On his tombstone he memorialized the major discoveries of his life, and he highlighted the epitaph with: "Camped at Yosemite, November 13, 1833."

Joe Walker and his men were the first whites to view magnificent Yosemite. Walker had the discovery carved on his tombstone.

John C. Fremont became famous through self-promotion rather than through the merits of his exploits.

ghostwrote eloquent and exciting "autobiographical" journals about her husband's travels. This is not to say that Captain Fremont lacked the courage, will, or wherewithal to survive in the worst conditions that nature could hurl at any man. It is simply that due to his shameless self-promotion, his exploits were remembered far longer than those of less literate and more humble men.

Aside from his connections, the most propitious thing that ever happened to Fremont in his grab for fame was a chance meeting with Christopher "Kit" Carson on a boat ride up the Missouri River in 1842. Even the self-absorbed Fremont could appreciate a man, however physically diminutive, like Kit Carson. "I was pleased with him and his manner of address at our first meeting," Fremont (actually his wife) later wrote. "He was a man of frank speech and address; quiet and unassuming."[34] The diffident Carson, the picture of humility, never considered himself half the Indian fighter that he truly was, and that suited Fremont fine, since he wanted no one on his expeditions who might try to steal the spotlight.

What resulted was an amicable blend of pompous headline grabbing and quiet pathfinding that, in the end, served them both well. Kit Carson did the real trailblazing and Fremont took most of the credit in his published journals. Interestingly, Fremont did come to genuinely like and respect Carson enough to give him the credit he deserved; sufficient credit to make the name "Kit Carson" synonymous with "Indian fighter"; eventually, more legends than true-life tales sprang up around his name. However, that was the case for many Indian fighters both east and west of the Mississippi. The young country was, after all, in search of its own particularly American heroes. And no group better supplied that need than the pathfinders, the fur trappers, the warriors—in short, the Indian fighters—especially when they were fighting Indians.

CHAPTER 4

Skirmishes and Single Warrior Combat in the East

Perhaps no form of human conflict symbolizes both its brutality and its dispute-settling potential as dramatically as single warrior combat, either in the context of matched pairs or small groups that split up to fight individually. Simply described, a representative of one group squares off against a representative of another (either by design or by accident) to settle their otherwise insoluble differences. Single warrior combat has ancient roots, with precedents including David and Goliath, Roman gladiators in the arena, armored knights jousting in medieval tournaments, swordplay between fencing musketeers, and pistol duels between gentlemen. Rarely, however, did it reach the ferocity generated when a white Indian fighter and an Indian brave clashed one-to-one.

"The Best Little Indian Fight Ever"

Daniel Boone's younger brother Squire sprinted for the closing gates of the Boonesborough stockade. There were Indians nearby, whooping in the woods, and he did not want to fight them alone. He heard shots fired, from both the log blockhouses and the black-green foliage to his flank. Clouds of white gunsmoke billowed out from both. He was at least a hundred yards from the gates; suddenly, footsteps trampling behind him made the distance seem all the farther. He

glanced back at a muscle-rippled Shawnee brave closing on him; he could almost smell the man's grease and paint.

Then Boone heard the cries, the shrill, shrieking shouts of the sweat-glistened warrior in pursuit, and they swelled to an explosion in his ears. He felt his own heart, the panting of his lungs; he knew he could not make the fort in time. Erupting with a war cry to match his opponent's, he spun around abruptly on his moccasined heels and rose up like a bear, cursing out a deep, guttural roar no bear could utter.

He whipped out his knife, a short sword, really, and swung it in the air with a whoop. The naked brave exploded into him with his tomahawk whirling and the two crashed to the shuddering earth. They rolled and tumbled, clutched and tore; they spit and bit and snarled. They strained, muscle against muscle, sinew against sinew, and soul against searing soul.

What took only seconds seemed a lifetime to Boone. The Indian bashed Boone's head wide open with his "hawk." Grappling and groping, he still managed to fight on. He made a wild upward thrust with his knife and felt the massive blade plunge in all the way to the hilt as if into the belly of a buck. But the Indian kept pounding Boone's head until his lights went dim, and the world seemed an aching distant place. Pain rippled from ear to ear. Somehow he kept twisting and jamming his knife ever inward and upward, sideways

Daniel and Squire Boone escape the Indians, but a friend is scalped. Such death-defying encounters did little to dampen the Boones' spirit for wanderlust.

and down. His whole hand went wet and warm until, at last, he sensed his opponent crumple and slide heavily to the ground.

Without remembering how, Squire Boone made it back to the fort, bleeding profusely from the head, nearly scalped. Probably trying to distance himself from the horror of the ordeal, he would later say casually of his single warrior combat that "it was the best little Indian fight ever. Both parties fought so well." [35]

What a Difference a Death Makes

Such respect for a fallen enemy was not uncommon among the Indian fighters. It was, in fact, a reflection of their own prowess if the men they killed were fierce opponents who, no doubt, would have bested another, lesser white man. One-to-one fighting provided the Indian fighters with a pure and true arena in which to prove themselves worthy of the woods. No one could diminish a man's courage and glory, as they might in full-scale battles, by saying that an Indian fighter had only contributed to a larger victory.

And so it was that men told, retold, exaggerated, and lied about the stories of their single warrior combat and generally left it to others to tell the tales of battles. Some even cut notches in knife grips, rifle stocks, and tomahawk handles to commemorate the personal victories they had won entirely on their own. Many took scalps for the same reason.

The status of a living enemy, however, could not be evaluated in the same way. An Indian too well respected in his own lifetime might create a fear in the Indian fighter that could only work against him in a duel. Usually, the more highly a frontiersman regarded an Indian in the caverns of his heart, the more he outwardly dehumanized and vilified him.

A Worthy Foe

The measure of any conqueror must depend on the measure of the enemy he conquers. James Smith, General Braddock's road builder captured by the Indians at Fort Duquesne, lived among his captors as a brave for five years and left a vivid testimony to the prowess of the warriors with whom the white frontiersmen struggled. As quoted in Voices from the Wilderness:

"I have often heard the British officers call the Indians undisciplined savages. But this is a capital mistake; they have all the essentials of discipline—they are under good command, punctual in obeying orders, they can act in concert by each man observing the motion or movement of his right-hand companion. They can perform various necessary maneuvers, either slowly, or as fast as they can run: form a circle or a semi-circle; also a hollow square. When they go into battle, they are not loaded or encumbered with many clothes, they commonly fight naked, save only the breech-cloth, leggings and moccasins. They are commonly well-equipped, and exceedingly active and expert in the use of arms.

Their officers plan, order, and conduct matters until they are brought into action; they will cheerfully unite in putting all directions into immediate execution. General orders are commonly given the time of battle, either to advance or retreat, and this is done by a shout or yell and then each man is to fight as if he were to gain the battle himself. Indians do not regard the number of white men against them. If they can only get them in a huddle, they will fight them ten to one.

They will send out their most active runners as spies, who will, when the wind is high, the sentinels cannot hear them crawling, slip past and view the camp. If they find the enemy encampment on a small piece of ground, and in close order, it greatly encourages them to make an attack; because if they can suddenly rush in around them, and get behind trees, they have frequently killed twenty to one."

In part, most Indian fighters displayed a cavalier attitude toward killing Indians, which often led to a callous disregard for the value of an Indian life. Once he killed his enemy, the greatness of his dead foe magically swelled to match and enhance his own, as reflected by the number of rivers, towns, mountains, and states named after slain or dispossessed Indians (Ohio, Mohawk, Muskingham, Miami, and thousands more across the country). Squire Boone's respect for the fight his opponent put up stands as evidence of that respect for the dead. The following accounts of single warrior combat illuminate the careless and cynical disrespect with which Indian fighters, by necessity, regarded the living.

A Joke on Young Jim

Dawn came up misty and bleak on Nutter's Fort at Clarksburg, Virginia (now West Virginia). Jesse Hughes, the chief Indian fighter there, had gone out the day before to scout the forested hills surrounding the fort and knew that Indians were about. Accordingly, he had gathered the nearby settlers within the tiny log palisade of the fort to await a possible attack.

Nerves were jumping, frustrations rising. After a sleepless night watch, an impatient youth by the name of Jim had had quite enough of waiting; and Hughes found him hurriedly loading his flintlock. Hughes, in his customary joking manner, asked the boy what he was doing and where he intended to go in such a bluster.

Jim snapped that he was going out to kill the turkey he heard gobbling on the hill just out in front of the stockade. He had decided that the Indians spotted the day before had moved on, probably down to Buckhannon Fort, and that the danger was over.

Smiling playfully, Hughes cocked his ear to the wind and listened for the turkey. And, sure enough, he heard it. It sounded like a big old tom to him, he said; surely they should not let it get away.

Fine, said Jim. And he started out the gate after it.

The affable Indian fighter grabbed his arm to stop him. Why didn't the boy let him go instead, he suggested to Jim. He added that he was a better shot than the boy and, thus, he should bag the bird. He promised that he would gladly turn the prize over to the boy upon his return.

A soldier views a fallen comrade. Such scenes raised a fierce desire for revenge among the Indian fighters.

Less than completely satisfied (he still felt cooped up in the little fort), Jim deferred to the master hunter and let him go after the still-gobbling bird. He was puzzled, though, when Hughes hopped over the back wall of the palisade and disappeared in the wrong direction to begin his tracking. Jim shrugged and decided that he would give Hughes first crack at the turkey but head out into the hills to hunt it on his own should he miss.

Before long, Jim heard one shot echo down from where the gobbler had been. He was disappointed. He knew that if Hughes had bagged the bird he would still be stuck inside the fort.

In mere minutes, the Indian fighter bounded through the front gate, but he carried no turkey. He was smiling, though, as if thoroughly satisfied. Jim chastised the scout for missing the shot, a shot, he claimed, he surely would have made.

Hughes just laughed out loud at this boy who so desperately wanted to be a man and said that he had gotten his quarry all right. From behind his back, he tossed a fresh scalp at Jim's feet and informed him what he had known all along: that the gobbling had come from a Delaware brave who had wanted nothing more than for Jim or someone equally inexperienced to come up hunting on his hill alone.

Young Jim, for his part, turned ashen and stumbled away, embarrassed by his impertinence and faint with the realization that

Simon Girty: Victim or Victimizer, White or Indian?

Someone aware of the horrendous experiences that Simon Girty suffered during his frontier childhood might have forgiven him for the many violent acts he later visited upon frontier settlers. As a small boy, he witnessed an Indian tomahawk his alcoholic father's head wide open, he watched his stepfather tortured and scalped, he saw his mother and brothers dragged off into captivity, and he himself was eventually enslaved by the Indians until he was eighteen years old. It is, therefore, conceivable that this early brutality shaped his own cruelty.

However, no white person anywhere on the frontier reserved any pity for Simon Girty, regardless of his background, for the enemies on whom he vented his pent-up frustrations were not Indians but Indian fighters and their families. He was a renegade, a skilled and fearless warrior who went over to the other side. Girty had no trouble winning the respect of the Indians. He led scores of successful raids against the whites during the 1780s and 1790s and also organized, inspired, and equipped them.

Jon Hale's *Trans-Allegheny Pioneers* quotes this motivational diatribe of Girty's: "Brothers! The Long Knives [whites] have overrun your country and usurped your hunting grounds. They have destroyed the cane, trodden down the clover, killed the deer and buffalo. Brothers, unless you rise in the majesty of your might and exterminate their whole race, you may bid adieu to the hunting grounds of your fathers."

His predictions may have been uncannily accurate and his leadership abilities considerable, but his name would be anathema up and down the frontier for generations. To frontier whites he was a turncoat, a traitor, the worst thing a white man could be. He was a renegade, a demonized sadist who tortured and murdered his own.

he had nearly danced with death. The wiry Hughes strode away, admired and appreciated by all those around him. There was no right or wrong. A danger had been quelled, an enemy killed, making their chances of survival all the better. No doubt the Indian would have felt the same had he won the fight.

A Scalp from Beyond the River

On another occasion, a party of some twenty Indians made an isolated raid on settlers in what is now central West Virginia. An enraged party of thirty white men led by their militia captain took off after them along a trail that was clearly headed for the Ohio River and safety 120 miles to the west. Jesse Hughes went along, of course. Nothing could keep him out of a scrape with the Indians, especially one to revenge the killings of friends whom he had sworn to protect.

Hughes knew a shortcut to the mighty Ohio that would have them lying in wait for the raiding party when they reached the river. Taking that shortcut, however, would mean giving up the hot pursuit of the braves just when it looked like they might be able to catch up with them. The militia captain's blood was up. Bravely yet foolhardedly he urged the party to stay on their current trail and slaughter the Indians wholesale. He even suggested that Jesse Hughes was a coward for not wanting to engage in a skirmish then and there. Jesse held his peace and reluctantly submitted to the captain's orders, especially since the man's fiery oratory had inspired the other men to cheers.

A few hours later, without having overtaken the Indians, the whites were faced with a descent of a precipitous ravine. Hughes sensed that this would be a perfect place for the braves to set up an ambush. And he sensed right. A noise, the cracking of a branch, split the air. It was an old ploy and one that nearly always worked. At the sudden sound, the frontiersmen all stopped in their tracks and looked. In that instant, with the white men frozen as perfect targets, the Indians on the opposite ridge opened fire and cut down two of them. Before their smoke had cleared, they had sped away into the noonday twilight of the primeval forest.

Stunned, confused, and rattled by the screams of their two dying friends, the frontiersmen were now ready to submit to Hughes's more seasoned leadership and follow him on his shortcut to the Ohio. They quick-stepped and ran for the next twelve hours, through the night without sleep, driven by Hughes and their consuming passion for vengeance, but the Indians were obviously doing the same. Hughes and the party reached the wide river shortly after the Indians, whose abandoned rafts could be seen floating downstream. If there was to be payback now, the whites were going to have to cross over, too. And cutting themselves off from "civilization" to enter Indian territory with a river at their backs was not something the exhausted party was prepared to do.

Scoffing, Hughes let them go their own way and leave the revenge they had been after to him alone. He took off on his own three miles upriver and crossed over on a hastily constructed driftwood raft. Arriving on the other side, he immediately set up camp, for night was falling swift and black. At dawn he picked up the Indians' trail and followed it ten miles west of the river, now outnumbered twenty to one. Discovering the Indian camp, he settled in beyond it and waited like a panther for an opportunity. One presented itself before long. Soon, all of the braves left to go hunting; all, that is, but one. He observed that single Indian, singing and

In the depths of the frontier, Indian fighters fool a group of Indians into ambushing a set of dummies made to look like them. Such ambushes were common among frontiersmen who imitated the stealthy guerrilla tactics of the Indians.

playing a musical instrument, frolicking by himself in false security. Hughes neither hesitated nor took needless chances. He crept up behind the singing warrior and shot him in the back of his head.

After a brutal scalping, Hughes snatched up his bloody prize and ran. And he did not stop running until he had made it back across the river and on to the Virginia fort. Once there, he boasted of his prowess and chided the men who had turned back. And, of course, he magnified and glorified the courage and the fighting abilities of the warrior he had killed across the Ohio.

Tales from an Even Darker Side

Some Indian fighters were callous, often committing as many savageries as the "savages"

they fought. A contemporary of Jesse Hughes who was also ranging through the wooded hills of present-day West Virginia returned to his fort bragging about his new pair of moccasins. When asked how and where he got the unusual footwear, he laughed coarsely and said that an Indian had given them to him. Actually, he had taken them from the Indian and done so in a most hideous manner. He had captured the brave, lashed him to a tree, and skinned him alive for the "leather."

The evil that these men carried out can be partially understood, though never justified, by the general tenor of the late 1700s. No less prominent a man than President Thomas Jefferson instructed his men on the frontier to "lift the hatchet against any tribe who [resists American expansion]. We will never lay it down until that tribe is exterminated, or is driven beyond the Mississippi."[36] The mandate seemed clear enough to the Indian fighters throughout the Appalachians and beyond although some carried it to unforgivably grotesque extremes.

Four Warriors—One at a Time

Even Lewis Wetzel did not have an atrocity-free record as far as fighting Indians was concerned, although his record of taking on armed braves singly is unblemished. Wetzel served as the chief Indian fighter around what is now Wheeling, West Virginia. His exploits rivaled, if not surpassed, those of his contemporary, Daniel Boone, and he would no doubt be as famous today as the Kentuckian had someone like John Filson chosen him as his subject.

Fame meant little, however, to Lewis Wetzel. He fought Indians for the sheer adventure of it. The fact that braves had killed his father and countless friends gave him the added incentive that only burning vengeance can provide.

Described by a friend as "daring where daring was the wiser part and prudent when discretion was valor's better self," his eyes were "piercing as the dagger's point, emitting, when excited, such fierce and withering glances as to cause the stoutest adversary to quail beneath their power."[37] Among his many forest skills, Wetzel had learned young how to run at full speed while loading his flintlock, a feat no one else, white or Indian, before or since, ever mastered. And on at least one occasion, that skill served him well.

When the Rifle Failed

Aside from his rifle, a man of the frontier relied heavily on three other weapons, all of which he could bring to bear on an enemy with the flick of a wrist. And the time it took him to flick his wrist was usually all the time he had. Whether walking a trail, riding on horseback, or standing guard on a lonely outpost, the Indian fighter kept his rifle loaded, primed, and half-cocked in order to meet a sudden threat, be it a gunshot, the flash of a knife, or a tomahawk swipe. But when he fired his one and only rifle shot, he usually did not have time to reload. That is when he brought out the rest of his arsenal.

He might first produce two flintlock dueling pistols from his belt and blast a .45-caliber hole through the chests of the first two braves to jump him. If more Indians were attacking, he threw down the pistols (which were loaded as were rifles) and drew his hunting knife, a wide, hilted blade of steel sometimes ten inches long. He could slash and cut an Indian with repeated short thrusts, but a killing penetration between a brave's ribs could cause the blade to get stuck.

If more than one assaulting Indian ever surrounded the Indian fighter and came at him from two or three angles, he pulled his tomahawk from the back of his belt and took on all comers. Perhaps his favorite of all hand-to-hand weapons, the honed, steel axblade could be swung in circles to fend off several at a time and still be directed into the skull of any Indian who became more isolated.

Despite skillful use of all these weapons, many a courageous and aggressive Indian fighter lost his life in the struggles in which he brought them to bear. And the reason is simple: The Indians whom he was fighting possessed all the same weapons along with their own skill and the courage to use them.

He and a friend were tracking down a missing horse. When they found it tied to a tree, Wetzel cautioned his friend not to approach it, as the scene had all the markings of an Indian trap. Disregarding the Indian fighter's warnings, the other man ran out to the horse and began untying it. Instantly the woods exploded in smoke and fire. Wetzel counted at least four shots, and the riddled condition of his friend's body confirmed as much.

Wetzel sprang away into the trees with the whooping braves close behind him. When the first brave came within tomahawk range, Wetzel turned and blew his chest apart with his single-shot rifle. Surely, the other three Indians must have thought he was easy prey now. The next fastest warrior came within closing distance, unaware that Wetzel had somehow managed to reload his gun on the run. Wetzel spun around again but had to grapple with the brave hand to hand for a moment. When he wrenched the end of his rifle away from the snarling Indian, he jammed it into the man's neck and nearly decapitated him with the blast. Still the other slower Indians kept up their pursuit and Wetzel ran on,

ramming, priming, and reloading once again. And once again he turned to face a tomahawk-swinging Indian and shot him dead in his stumbling tracks. At that, the fourth Indian stopped and fled back down the path. Wetzel heard him crying as he went, "No catch that man—him gun always loaded!"[38]

Iron Man Before His Time

Indian fighters who could not reload their rifles at a sprint had no alternative to fighting when outnumbered but running and swimming and riding horseback; that is, getting themselves to safety by whatever means available. Usually, however, it was the running that saved them; thus their physical condition was of the utmost importance. One western Virginia Indian fighter by the name of Jacob Reger was in such peak condition. He was employed by Buckhannon Fort (now Buckhannon, West Virginia) to scout and provide an early warning system to the settlers of approaching Indians. These duties required long, lone excursions as far distant as 150 miles that lasted for days, if not weeks.

Lewis Wetzel vengefully pursued Indians after his father and many friends had been ambushed and killed. Wetzel is famous for his ability to load a flintlock rifle while running at full speed.

On one such trek, Reger spied a large war party of Delaware braves crossing the Ohio River in a fleet of canoes. He knew he could not delay them in any way so went to work in the capacity of long-distance, early warning runner. Spotted by the painted braves before he could get away, he was said to have run pursued for 125 miles nonstop. The Indians had to rest at intervals, allowing him to pull enough ahead to reach his settlement a couple of hours ahead of the war party.

Exhausted after what had been a twenty-four-hour marathon, Reger still managed to fulfill his other obligations as Buckhannon Fort's professional Indian fighter. He oversaw the rounding up of all the scattered settlers within the walls of the small log stockade and arranged defenses and supplies for what might be a long siege. To add a little offensive sting to the preparations, he set up an ambush in the woods for the approaching Indians, manned by several of the ablest settlers. As if on cue, the braves appeared where he said they would and the white men shot several of them, causing the survivors to redirect their attack to a less well-prepared fort elsewhere. Once again, Jacob Reger had proven his worth to the community who paid his wage, although it is doubtful that he was thinking much about the money just then. As the day closed, his foremost concern must have been getting a good night's sleep.

A Boone for a New Generation

Second only to Daniel Boone in the annals of American Indian fighters was a man named David Crockett (he never referred to himself as Davy, nor did anyone who knew him). David Crockett grew up in Tennessee around the turn of the nineteenth century feeding on stories of Daniel Boone and other

David Crockett, the Indian fighter who later defended the Alamo, is perhaps the most well-remembered frontiersman today.

Indian fighters who were "civilizing" the frontier at that time. By the time Crockett came of age in the new century's first decade,

Boone had settled much of Kentucky but much of the trans-Allegheny frontier still remained untamed and ripe for the conquering. However, Crockett had just one incident during that time that even remotely qualified as a bout of single warrior combat akin to the many attributed to Daniel Boone. Even though the event was more an abomination than a victory, it was something that the self-promoting Crockett could later exaggerate into a great feat of courage and fighting ability.

Crockett was leading a small party of Tennessee Indian fighters and friendly Indians against a camp of hostile Creeks in Alabama. He had spotted their dwellings and begun to devise an attack plan when the friendly Indians let out a surprise-ruining set of victory screams some distance away from his position. Knowing that his party would be revealed to the enemy if he did not quickly quash the ruckus, he bounded off into the swampy woods to silence his allies.

Once there, he saw the source of their celebration. His two Indians had captured and beheaded two Creek braves after finding out from them that the camp had been evacuated. Feeling safe from attack, Crockett did the only appropriate thing he felt was left to him in the situation: He joined the two living Indians in smashing the heads of the dead corpses. Many Indians believed that an enemy's body in the after-life could be damaged by mutilating his dead body on this side of eternity.

Whatever his reasons, David Crockett later claimed that he had helped kill them in a fair fight. He engaged belligerent Indians in a few other instances but always with support from several others. No one, though, can ever deny the bravery and self-sacrifice he exhibited in the gloriously defiant defeat at the Alamo. But as a single combat warrior, David Crockett fell far short of the legends he helped to create.

However, so many others, both white and Indian, did not.

Face to Face in the West

Tom Fitzpatrick was a tough, ornery-eyed but educated Irishman who came to America as a young man to make his way in the world. And make his way he did, from New York to Ohio to Indiana and finally to St. Louis, where he worked as a bookkeeper until he answered the following advertisement for fur trappers in a local newspaper:

TO ENTERPRISING YOUNG MEN

The subscriber wishes to engage ONE HUNDRED MEN, to ascend the river Missouri to its source, there to be employed for one, two, or three years—For particulars, inquire of Major Andrew Henry, near the Lead Mines, in the county of Washington (who will ascend with and command the party) or to the subscriber at St. Louis.[39]

Young Fitzpatrick signed on, lying about his knowledge (or lack thereof) of the fur trapping business, but he learned the trade quickly from the likes of Jedediah Smith, Jim Bridger, and other boys and young men who had signed on with similar lies. In a few years, Tom Fitzpatrick had not only learned the ways of the Rocky Mountains but had become a feared Indian fighter in his own right, a survivor of countless duels with the natives. On at least one occasion, however, he found himself alone against a dozen savage Blackfoot braves and it appeared that not even his considerable combat skills would be able to save him from a grisly death.

A Leap of Faith

The mounted Blackfeet spotted him in the Yellowstone River area and gave chase, screaming loudly enough to part the billowy clouds overhead. Fortunately, he was riding a particularly spirited animal and he pushed it hard to gain a little ground. The Indians were thinking one step ahead of Fitzpatrick, though. They drove him toward an escape-proof cliff. He pulled up just short of a one-hundred-foot plunge into the rocky river below and shot a glance back at the rapidly closing braves.

This was it, he was sure. Certainly, there could be no escaping this time. He would either die pierced by a swarm of arrows or suffer the endless agony of torture back at the savages' village. Those were his only options. Or were they? He studied the raging rapids far below. Could he possibly survive the fall? Probably not, but he knew he would certainly die if he remained on the bluff another instant.

As quickly as he thought it, Fitzpatrick gritted his teeth and rammed his spurs into the horse's sides. The beast screamed and reared back in protest. He spurred it again and again until it leaped off the cliff in a wild-eyed, neighing panic. Seconds later, years later, what seemed to him a lifetime later, the thrashing animal crashed into the racing waters below, banging against rocks and logs and snags. The Irishman flew out of the saddle and plunged headlong into the icy depths, surfacing off and on with chokes and gasps and gags.

The hide of the deer served as a staple for Indian fighters when it came time for them to make pouches, bags, packs, gun cases, knife sheaths, and especially clothing. But before they could begin to fashion all of these necessities, the frontiersmen had to first harvest the raw material: the buckskin itself. The mighty and majestic buck, or male deer, was not an easy quarry to bring down, particularly when the Indian fighter had only one shot to fire before he had to reload. If he did not make a clean kill through the heart or lungs on his first attempt, he might have to track the sloppily wounded animal for miles before bagging it, assuming that he could bag it at all.

Hunters acknowledged and respected the defensive sensitivities of the deer, its keen ability to smell, hear, and see any discrepancy in the natural order of its habitat. Accordingly, they had to approach the game from downwind to avoid scent detection, remain absolutely silent, and step glacially, if at all, in order not to have his movement picked up. Frontiersmen often managed this by hiding in bushes near watering holes or by camouflaging themselves in tree perches called stands that afforded them the added advantage of being above the deer's natural angle of sight.

If a buck came by and if the hunter's overanxious "buck fever" did not cause him to rush his shot, and if that shot proved instantly fatal, then the harvesting could commence. The hunter began by tying the buck's two hind hooves together, throwing the rope over a strong tree branch, and hoisting the heavy carcass to a hanging position. With his butcher's knife, he would slit the buck open from anus to throat and scoop the guts onto the ground. He next slit the inside of the animal's legs and around its neck, cutting loose the connective tissues securing the hide to the muscles until it was possible to pull it away from the bloody carcass, and claim the animal's skin for his own.

And still, there was so much left to do.

A hunter dries deer carcasses in the sun. The deer was hunted not only for food but also for its hide, which was made into buckskin garments.

Blackfoot warriors were feared by the Indian fighters because of their courage, skill, and intense resentment of whites.

He clutched at the saddle of the thrashing horse, straining and struggling for his rifle. He finally pulled it out of the saddle holster, fully loaded as it always was, and grabbed it by the full-cocked trigger. The mighty weapon exploded in a fury of smoke and fire and lead, blowing a gaping hole through his left hand. Agonized, seared, burned red and raw, Fitzpatrick managed to splash his way to the shore. He wrapped the shreds of his hand in a buckskin rag and took cover behind a rock.

Fighting Wounded

Fitzpatrick watched the Blackfeet climb down the cliff to collect whatever trophies they could from the dead white man they were sure lay at the bottom. Wincing in pain, eyes blurred by sweat, water, and suffering,

he managed to reload his rifle and took careful aim at the unsuspecting brave in the lead. He squeezed off a thunder-clapping, shoulder-kicking round and watched that Indian go down. He reloaded by the time the second Indian had made it across the river and he killed that one, too. He did not wait for a third to make himself a target. He took off into the darkened woods behind him with the other braves in hollering pursuit.

Treating the killer of their two friends with a new measure of respect, the remaining Indians kept their distance, however, and finally gave up altogether and let Fitzpatrick go his way, possibly concerned that he might double back and set up another ambush. Merely postponing their revenge, the braves knew that they would be able to identify him later by the mangled left hand they had seen. In fact, the Blackfeet eventually gave him a name that would set him apart the rest of his

Meriwether Lewis shoots at Blackfoot braves as they scatter while stealing the expedition's horses.

life. Old Broken Hand, they called him, and his scalp became forever prized.

An Unfortunate Beginning

One of the first fatal skirmishes between U.S. citizens and the Indians in the West occurred in 1806 during the waning days of the Lewis and Clark expedition (an endeavor considered by many to be the first thrust of American Indian fighters into the frontier west of the Mississippi River). Meriwether Lewis had taken three men from the main party to explore the mountains of what is now northwestern Montana. This was Blackfoot Indian territory, he knew, and he had already discovered that they were not favorably disposed toward the upstart United States of America.

He had, likewise, already formed strong opinions of the Blackfeet as his journal entry prior to the fight indicated:

> They are a vicious, lawless, and rather an abandoned set of wretches. I wish to avoid an interview with them if possible. Finding us weak should they happen to be numerous, the Blackfeet will most

probably attempt to rob us of our arms and baggage. I will take every possible precaution to avoid them if possible. We consider ourselves extremely fortunate in not having met with these people.[40]

The four men's fortune expired, though, in the late afternoon of July 26. They spotted eight young Blackfoot braves who quickly spotted them. After a tense initial meeting, which nearly escalated into an exchange of bullets and arrows, Lewis used his usual gifts and diplomacy to get the Blackfeet to camp with them for the night. It had always been his desire to befriend as many tribes as possible with the hope that they would begin trading with the Americans instead of the British and, around the fire that night, he gave these braves his best sales pitch. He went to sleep thinking that perhaps he had laid the groundwork for a lasting and profitable peace. At dawn, however, the angry shouts of one of his men splintered that hope forever.

Caught in the Act

The Blackfoot braves were trying to steal the white men's rifles, an offense tantamount to murder among frontiersmen. In seconds, the entire camp was bursting with fistfights, wrestling matches, biting, and eye gouging between the four whites and eight Indians. The braves who could get away scattered in all directions, some to steal the horses and others to make off with the guns. One of Lewis's men chased down a rifle-robbing Indian and plunged a huge knife into the boy's heart.

While the other three men tried to chase down the horses, Lewis, enraged at the betrayal, went after the two Indians holding his own mount. They were little more than teenagers, he could tell, but they were armed with bows, knives, and a musket of their own, and they had taken up an ambush position behind a boulder. Fully exposed, Lewis strode straight for the boys with his rifle at the ready. His rage was surging far ahead of his fear. Using angrily gesticulated sign language, he demanded the return of his animal. When the Indians did not comply, he fired and felled one of the boys. The fight was not quite over, though. The wounded Blackfoot managed to get off a surprisingly accurate musket round before collapsing. "Being bareheaded," Lewis said, "I felt the wind of his bullet very distinctly."[41]

With two Blackfeet dead and the others fleeing for reinforcements, Lewis and his men rapidly broke camp and sped away on the horses they had been able to recover. They did not stop riding until early the next morning and even then they risked only a short rest. They had been lucky, Lewis knew, to get out of Blackfoot country alive, but he did not comprehend the ramifications of that first Indian fight for the United States: one hundred years of nearly constant strife with the Blackfeet, who swore in 1806 never to make peace with the trespassing Americans.

Fast Food

Lewis's party had lost all their food to the Indians during the fight and, when far enough away to stop, they killed a buffalo and made a meal of it. The buffalo had always been a favorite source of "fast food" among frontiersmen and Indians on the move, and certain customs of killing and eating them had evolved into common practice.

If the herd was grazing in a more or less stationary position, the hunter would drape himself in a buffalo robe for camouflage and carefully approach downwind from the animals to carry any scent of himself (which was usually considerable) away from the sensitive-

A frontiersman poses with a buffalo he downed. The easily obtainable buffalo was considered the fast food of the Plains.

nosed animals. A well-placed shot between the breast and the shoulder could send the two-thousand-pound beast down. If, however, the hunter missed the target, it might take two dozen shots and thirty minutes to whittle the six-footer to the ground, and at any time during its raucous demise, the victim could thrash around enough to launch the entire herd into a quaking stampede, especially if any of the other animals caught wind of the hunter's vile aroma.

A successful kill, though, could easily and rapidly feed large numbers of people either on the spot, in a camp, or back at a village. Famished men in the field would first cut out the tongue, which they considered a delicacy, and eat it raw, saliva, dirt, and all, after seasoning it with a dose of gunpowder. The hump went next, fatty flavored and tender, and then the intestines, which they preferred lightly seared. It was not uncommon to find some whites and Indians traveling with buffalo guts festooned from their neck and shoulders in anticipation of the next campfire they might be able to build. The meat, of course, was what they consumed the most of, either raw or cooked on a stick, and they often finished their meal drinking the liquid treats: blood from the heart, melted fat, and the juices, called cider, from within the intestines of the butchered beast.

Back in camp (especially an extended winter camp), they would cut strips of the meat, soak it in salt brine, and hang it out in the sun to dry into jerky, an important source of quick rations to be consumed on the trail. Another popular preparation of buffalo trail rations was pemmican, a combination of buffalo meat and fat pounded together and dried into patties.

Buckskin: The Tanning

Before the hide of a buck could be cut and sewn into the many products for which the Indian fighters would ultimately use it, it first had to be prepared, or tanned. The arduous chore usually fell to their Indian wives if they had one or more. Often, though, the Indian fighters lived alone or with other white men so they had to master and perform the tasks themselves.

The untreated hide had to first be soaked through with water, stretched out on a broad log or a rock, and scraped with a sharpened bone implement on both sides: on the inside to remove adhering fat and flesh and on the outside to remove the hair. This step alone could take a full day of knuckle-busting, joint-aching scrubbing and scraping and always made the thought of "packing a squaw" seem more appealing.

Next, the tanner would take the brain of the buck, which he had carefully cut out of its skull, cook it into a mush, and knead it evenly into all of the hide's surfaces. This had the effect of softening and whitening the skin and was presumably no more noxious a task than gutting the deer in the first place.

Finally, the Indian fighter hung the hide over a low tree limb and built a wet, smoldering fire beneath it for the purpose of smoking it. Smoking darkened the buckskin to a hue that blended into the forest and mountain colors. Hides used for making clothing or accoutrements to be worn in the desert would be smoked for a shorter time. Smoking also served to waterproof the buckskin by drawing out natural oils from deep within the hide.

And now, with the tanning done, all that remained was the cutting and sewing of the "cloth."

Berries could be added to the mix to make one of the Indians' and Indian fighters' favorite treats. When rations ran out, however, and starvation threatened, Indian fighters routinely boiled and ate their moccasins, buckskin fringe, dogs, horses, ants, crickets, snakes, and lizards if they could catch them.

Like Mosquitoes They Swarmed

All thoughts of food faded, though, when white men encountered hostile Indians. Their reserves of adrenaline and fear-fed energy flushed away any hunger pangs. Even while in the presence of the most primitive of Indians, the desert-dwelling Diggers, travel could be hazardous to whites unfortunate enough to encounter them.

The Diggers barely survived in the arid wastelands of western Utah and eastern California, functioning at the Stone Age level. They had earned their name because, when hungry, they dug for roots, insects, and lizards and hunted small animals with spears. Long despised and abused by other more advanced Indians, the diminutive Diggers occupied the only land that no one else even wanted to cross, until now.

In 1833, the respected Indian fighter Joe Walker was leading an expedition of forty mountain men to California when he first encountered the Diggers. The white men found their camps and trails buzzing with them, and they stole everything they could scurry off with. Walker had frustrated his party by forbidding them to kill any of the Diggers. There was no reason to start a fight with them, he said, when they would be out of their territory in a few days.

However, more and more of the Diggers began to surround Walker's expedition both in camp and when traveling during the day. Walker estimated that nearly one thousand of them had assembled, and one night he ordered fortifications built. The tension increased when his hunters broke down and killed two or three of the Diggers, further fomenting a showdown. "Dancing and singing with the greatest glee," according to one of the mountain men with Walker, they agitated for a fight, but still Walker would not start one.

Surely, he thought, these primitive Indians would stop pestering his men if they were somehow made aware of his modern firepower. He called a truce and set up a demonstration of how his weapons could devastate a beaverskin target. Yet even this did not impress at least one hundred of the Diggers who massed to attack the next morning. An Indian fighter with Walker reported, "This greatly excited Captain Walker, who was naturally of a cool temperament, and he gave orders for the charge, saying that there was nothing equal to a good start in such a case."[42]

The Indian fighters wiped out some forty Diggers in the onslaught. The Diggers, for their part, seemed to have learned from this second demonstration and faded into the waves of the salt-blanched desert. Not all of the Diggers were such quick studies, however. On Walker's return trip through the same area, he was compelled to make an object lesson of another fourteen, whose stealing, mocking, wheedling, and cajoling caused them to pay for the repeat instruction with their lives.

Vengeance, Revenge, and Revenge Again

Not all Diggers, however, lost their lives fighting. By 1850, several semi-retired Indian fighters had settled in California on the edge of Digger territory and had established cattle ranches. They "employed" (or, more accurately, enslaved) the Diggers as cattle herders. In at least one instance, two aged Indian fighters by the names of Stone and Kelsey routinely practiced extreme cruelty in their "employee management."

According to one of the Diggers, "About twenty people died during the winter from starvation. From severe whipping, four died. A nephew of an Indian lady who was living with Stone was shot to death by Stone. The Indians suffered whipping and the tying of their hands together with rope. The rope was then thrown over the limb of a tree and then drawn up until the Indians' toes barely touched the ground and let them hang there for hours. Such punishment occured two or three times a week. And many men and women died from fear and starvation."[43]

Under conditions such as these, it does not seem surprising that a band of Diggers rose up and murdered Stone and Kelsey in their rough-hewn ranch house. And perhaps it is no less surprising that U.S. Army troops quickly moved in and retaliated by murdering over one hundred Digger men, women, and children in what came to be known as the Bloody Island Massacre of 1850.

One Route Closes and Another . . .

Another of the legendary pathfinders of the West was too devout a Christian to murder helpless Indians. And while Jedediah Smith may have opened up more of the North American continent than even Lewis and Clark (including California, the desert Southwest, and the Pacific Northwest), his prowess at fighting armed ones stands open to question. In the years between 1823 and 1831,

Smith engaged in four significant encounters with various Indian groups, and he and his men came out the losers each time. There can be no doubt as to the mountain man's individual bravery in combat, but perhaps his judgment faltered when it came to avoiding fights in the first place.

The first defeat, however, cannot be blamed on any of Smith's decisions. He was simply a hired frontiersman under William Ashley when that retired general's riverborne expedition fell under the attack of the Arikara Indians far up the Missouri River in 1823. The general made the mistake of leaving twenty-three of his fifty men onshore one night, including Smith, despite indications that the nearby Arikara were understandably agitated by the white men's presence. When the gray dawn faded in, the Indians killed fifteen of the shore party and maimed another eight.

After fifteen panicked and bloody minutes, the skirmish was over. Ashley retreated downstream to lick his wounds. Jedediah Smith was one of the few onshore to survive unscathed and, later, to grasp the full ramifications of the loss. For some time to come, he realized, the all-important Missouri River would be closed to white boat traffic. Another route into the West would have to be found, an overland route supplied by pack trains of horses and mules, and he determined to be one of those to blaze it.

A Hard Lesson Learned

Four years later, Smith was extending that route into California, a near mythical land as yet unexplored by Americans. His party of nineteen was struggling through the desiccated desert of southeastern California when Indians struck him in force for the second time. They were Mojave Indians this time,

Buckskin: The Finished Product

Once the buckskin hides were harvested and tanned, the Indian fighter could then fashion the raw material into the clothing and accoutrements that he needed in order to survive in the wilds of the forests, mountains, and deserts. Foremost among these necessities was clothing; by cutting and sewing the pieces of deer hide together, he was able to protect himself from the harshest elements east and west of the Mississippi River.

Using his knife and an awl (a forged cylindrical spike sharpened at one end to perform like a needle), the frontiersman could manufacture his own buckskin shirt by cutting a long, wide poncho of deer leather with a head hole in the center. He sewed fringed sleeves onto this torso section and laced up its sides with rawhide. To protect his legs, he did not fashion breeches with a seat but fringed, full-length leggings that laced up and attached to a rawhide string around his waist. A buckskin flap or loincloth protected his genitals and buttocks beneath his thigh-length shirt. For footwear, he cut and laced up form-fitting pieces of buckskin into top and bottom sections to make moccasins capable of quiet, cushioned foot travel.

In winter, the Indian fighter needed to protect his hands from the cold, so he sewed together the two halves of a mitten to custom fit them. He was careful to cut a slit in the inside of his right buckskin mitten to allow his trigger finger a quick and easy escape. He made sheathes for his knife and tomahawk, too, and a belt with which to secure them. He also fashioned a flintlock mechanism sleeve to keep the priming powder in his flash pan dry, a fringed, saddle-borne rifle case, and rawhide hobbles to restrict his horse's legs while he slept.

So far from civilization and the amenities factory manufacturing could provide, the Indian fighter readily mastered the ageless and arguably superior clothing and accoutrement-making skills of his enemy. It is telling that even when the rendezvous and trading posts were able to offer the mountain man the fabric and cloth of the "civilized" East, most still preferred to wear the same buckskins that they had worn for years.

swift runners with poison-tipped arrows who sucked the "cider" out of animal intestines when traversing waterless tracts. They were a crafty group who lured Smith's expedition into a sense of complacency with a feigned display of hospitality.

As soon as the Mojaves saw that Smith had divided his force to cross a nearby river, they swarmed over the ten left behind. All of these men suffered the sickening fate that only rattlesnake-venomed arrows can induce, plunging into vomiting and convulsive hallucinations. Smith and the others made their way to a sandbar, albeit one still connected to the Mojaves' side of the river. They hastily constructed a breastwork of cane and reeds and, as Smith wrote in his journal, "fastened our butcher knives with cords to the ends of light poles so as to form tolerable lances and thus poorly prepared, we waited."[44]

The surviving nine had only five rifles among them. But they fired them much farther and straighter than the Mojaves had ever imagined possible and, dropping the two lead braves, they drove the Indians back and managed to escape when night fell. For

Jedediah Smith encountered Mojave Indians like these who were bent on killing Smith and his men for invading their territory.

the second time the great trailblazer had met the enemy in tribal force, and for the second time he had to count himself among the losers. This time, however, the fault was his own and he vowed never to trust Indian "hospitality" again.

The Lesson Continues

Despite increased vigilance, Smith's party met its final demise in the rainy forests of Oregon six months later. Smith and two of his men had gone ahead of the rest to scout out a possible trail to Fort Vancouver, Washington. With his force once again split up, the Kelawatset Indians on whose ground they now traveled ambushed the larger party and killed fifteen out of sixteen. The tally for Jedediah Smith's expeditions over the past three years did not bode well for his reputation as an expedition leader. Out of a total of thirty-three men whom he had led into California and beyond, twenty-six had been killed by the Indi-

ans. Two others had lost faith in him altogether and deserted at Fort Vancouver. Though none doubted his personal courage and integrity, his luck and his judgment were in question.

Fittingly, this legendary mountain man and explorer eventually met the same fate as did so many of those who followed him. In 1831, while leading a trading expedition down the Santa Fe Trail, he allowed himself to be surrounded, alone, by Comanche braves at a water hole. They perforated him with gunfire but not before he brought down the chief who was leading them. He was thirty-two years old and already renowned throughout the West. The posthumous publication of his journal secured him his rightful place in the history of U.S. expansion.

The Indians who killed him no doubt pillaged his saddlebags in search of the two white man's items they coveted most (aside from his rifle), whiskey and tobacco. They would have been disappointed, though, for Jedediah Smith neither drank nor smoked. It is likely that they would have taken out their frustration on his beloved Bible, which he read daily, and cast it to the bloody sand.

Modest Men Tell Few Tales

According to a newspaper reporter who met him, Jim Bridger was "tall—six feet at least—muscular, without an ounce of superfluous flesh to impede its force or exhaust its elastic-ity. His cheek bones were high, his nose hooked or aquiline, the expression of his eyes mild and thoughtful, that of his face grave almost to solumnity."[45] His friend Jedediah Smith gave him the nickname "Old Gabe" because he reminded the ardent Bible reader of the archangel Gabriel. Perhaps it was Bridger's sincere humility, a rare trait among Indian fighters, that gave him the air of an angel. It certainly must account for why so few tales of his Indian fighting have survived.

That Old Corn Likker

Beverage alcohol was in widespread use in America in the eighteenth and nineteenth centuries, especially on the frontier. The enormous strains and stresses of daily survival in the wilds required potent relief. Brown Betty, sour mash, moonshine, and white lightning were all names given to various homemade inebriants guaranteed to keep a man's morale high at the end of a hard day, and any man with the skills to manufacture it quickly became well regarded by denizens of the woods. One aging "shiner" shared his secrets for conjuring "corn likker" this way, according to R. E. Dabney's *Mountain Spirits:*

> You git your barrel, whatever you're going to put your mash (unsprouted corn) in. If you're going to put up a whole lot, git you a sixty-gallon barrel, and put 9½ bushels of the mash in for every 1½ bushels of malt (corn soaked until it sprouts) and throw in a handful of bread yeast. Stir it all together and let it set three days (during which time the mixture ferments, producing alcohol as a by-product). Then put it in your still (an enclosed copper pot with a coiled tube running down from its top). Put it

on the fire and go to burnin' it. Put something under thar to catch your whiskey in.

Because alcohol boils before water does, the alcohol vapor drifts up into the coil first and distills into liquid as it winds its way down the cooling tube. "So you got it coiling around and around and your whiskey comes out of the tube. You've got to watch it, when it gits down kinda weak, your supposed to quit. Doublin' back, we call it, you catch a little and put it back in the boiler for the next batch. Doublin' back, boy, it's pure dee alkeehol then!"

One steady customer extolled the virtues of the moonshiner's commodity, saying, "Everybody took it. It brought out kind feelings of the heart, made men sociable, and in them days everybody invited everybody that come around them to partake in this wholesome beverage."

Perhaps, though, an old folk saying of the time best summed up the high regard in which the "fire water" was held:

> Here's to Old Corn Likker,
> Whitens the teeth,
> Perfumes the breath,
> And makes childbirth a pleasure.

Although Bridger shared many episodes confirming his skills as a scout, pathfinder, fur trapper, storyteller, whitewater man, and even farmer, it seems that he chose not to boast about the incidents during which he took the lives of the Indians. A soldier who worked with him said, "He never in my presence vaunted himself, about his own personal actions. He never told about how brave he was, nor how many Indians he had killed."[46] Perhaps his restraint was due to the fact that he often lived among the Indians, respected them, and remained faithfully married to his Indian wife for most of his adult life. In any case, it would seem to be an admirable trait, though one that has denied history full access to his experiences.

One tale to come down, however, involved a small party of Blackfeet who attempted to deceive Bridger and his men with a false offer of peace. "Old Gabe" sallied forth alone to smoke the peace pipe with the Blackfoot chief. Face-to-face, the chief grabbed the barrel of Bridger's rifle and cracked his head open with a tomahawk. Gunfire and bowstring twangs sounded out, and the chief galloped away on his horse. Bridger, dazed and bleeding, stumbled back to his side and joined in what became an hours-long skirmish. During the fight, he took two arrows in his shoulder, one of which remained embedded for three painful years until he could find a surgeon skilled enough to cut it out, without, of course, any anesthetic.

Unlike other Indian fighters, Jim Bridger never bragged about killing Indians.

A Good Friend and a Bad Enemy

Christopher "Kit" Carson was not a man to be confused with those who loved the Indian. A bantamweight scrapper from an early age, he had seriously violated the law at sixteen by running away from his obligatory apprenticeship to a Missouri saddler. Working his way back and forth across the West in pack trains and trapping expeditions, he fell under the tutelage of several bloodthirsty Indian haters and, inspired by them and the general tenor of the day, he killed his first Indian while still a teen.

As a fur trapper and mountain man, he saw no reason to stop the killing. He quickly earned a reputation as a "plain, simple, unostentatious man with a voice as soft as a woman's" but one who would "rip the guts"[47] out of his enemies, be they Indians or loud-mouth, bullying white men.

During one trappers' rendezvous, he dueled with flintlock pistols on horseback with one such white bully, a man Carson himself said "made a practice of whipping every man he was displeased with and that was nearly all."[48] At close range, the bully's bullet missed; Carson's shattered the big man's arm. Only loud and pitiful begging by the bully at the little man's feet kept Carson from finishing him off. And no further bullying occurred.

A Thin Line Between Bravery and Barbarism

In 1833, when Carson was winter trapping with Tom "Old Broken Hand" Fitzpatrick's party, fifty Crow Indians stole nine of their horses. Carson wrote:

In the morning we discovered sign of the Indians and twelve of us took the trail

Famed Indian fighter Kit Carson had a reputation for getting back at his enemies—both white and Indian.

of the Indians and horses. . . . We found them and when we thought they were all asleep, six of us crawled toward the horses and got them. . . . Then we decided to let the consequences be ever so fatal. . . . We opened a deadly fire, each ball taking its victim, and escaped. . . . Our suffering from the cold was soon forgotten, having sent many a redskin to his long home.[49]

In a representative display of both sides of Kit Carson's personal nature, he and just one other man set out to punish thirty Piutes who had murdered a young Mexican boy's parents. They found them at dawn after a twenty-four-hour ride through the scorching Mojave Desert. The Piutes were feasting on a

Kit Carson single-handedly wards off a group of Indians and rescues a fallen comrade. Carson's daring exploits against the Indians are still recognized today.

stolen horse and were temporarily separated from their weapons. In a surge of adrenalized rage, Carson and his partner charged the thirty Indians, shooting down two and scattering the rest. Before the Indians realized that there were only two attackers, Carson had scalped the two stricken braves, only one of whom was actually dead. The unostentatious little man with the voice as soft as a woman's brutally sliced his knife completely around the skull of the brave still screaming, ripped off his hair with a mighty yank, and capped the atrocity by leaving him to die slowly in the sun.

Captain John C. Fremont, whose journals would make his scout, Kit Carson, world fa-mous, called the incident, "the boldest which the annals of Western adventure can present."[50] Fremont's German cartographer disagreed in his journal, asking rhetorically, "Are these whites not much worse than the Indians?"[51]

While a rare man such as this cartographer occasionally protested the manner in which Indian fighters such as Kit Carson dispatched their Indian enemies, no one ever complained when they eliminated the most powerful and fierce of their opponents. These were foes so dangerous and terrifying to all men of the wilderness, white and Indian, that the riddance of one even reasonably nearby brought a unanimous sigh of relief.

6 The Other Enemies

During the late eighteenth and early nineteenth centuries, black bears inhabited the eastern woodlands and grizzly bears inhabited the western mountains in numbers nearly as great as those of the Indians themselves. Certainly they could be counted upon to do at least as much damage to an Indian fighter as any brave could. And adding to the mystique and horror of a bear attack was the understanding that the bear would usually eat its victim and, in most cases, do so while the person was still alive and screaming.

Lords of the Forest

Black bears have not changed in the last two hundred years. Then as now, they generally weighed four to five hundred pounds and stood six feet tall when reared on their hind legs. With a swipe of a paw, a black bear can render a man unconscious and be devouring him when he awakens. Its knifelike claws can scoop out its victim's intestines or rip off his face. Black bears climb trees after their quarry and have been known to overtake the fastest of runners, especially on an uphill course best suited to its long hind legs. And if that were not enough, the ursine beasts are able to simply roll over on their victims and rupture their internal organs like so many bursting balloons.

One unfortunate Indian, while in the process of besting a white frontiersman in a desperate bout of single warrior combat, stumbled into some underbrush. "It so happened," the white man later wrote, "was it Providence?—that a large she-bear had made her bed underneath the roots, where the ferocious beast was then suckling her cubs. As the astonished savage arose to his feet, the furious bear sprang upon him, and with a terrible hug, grasped him in her powerful arms, the Indian giving an unearthly yell from the great pain."[52]

The white man ran for his life, saved as it was by the angered she-bear. He returned the next day to the site to find the body of the Indian. Most likely the mother bear had eaten heartily of the young brave and dragged his carcass away for future dining, forever impressing the Indian fighter with how vicious the bear had been to the brave and how merciful God had been to him.

One Who Sought the Bear

Simply because the black bear could run so fast, climb so high, and fight so ferociously even when wounded, any person who killed one received the deep appreciation of the nearby settlers for ridding the woods of a dangerous predator. However, the benefits did not end there. The bear hunter's status in the community skyrocketed for possessing the skills, courage, and strength required to overcome such a monstrous beast.

A Man, His Dogs, and a Bear

It was winter and blue-cold but David Crockett's buckskins were soaked through with sweat from hours of trotting after bear tracks. At last, his yelping dogs caught the scent and treed a swatting bear. Crockett shot the animal twice, but when it hit the snow-packed earth it still managed to maul a couple of his shrieking hounds and chase him to within a heartbeat of his own life before going to ground in a four-foot crevice. Crockett could not get a clear shot at it down there so he

David Crockett with his hounds. A true frontiersman, Crockett often hunted solo with his dogs.

reached his reloaded rifle blindly into the protective ditch and squeezed off a third clapping round that merely nicked the bear's leg. That only served to bring it charging out in a rage to mangle another couple of dogs before thundering back down into its hideaway. Crockett realized that if he was to make this bear his prize, he was going to have to get uncomfortably close to it.

Crockett later wrote, "I got down, and my dogs got in before it and kept its head towards them, until I went to the other side of the crevice and got along up to it; and placing my hand on its rump, felt for his shoulder. I made a lunge with my long knife and fortunately stuck him right through the heart."[53]

Fortunately, indeed, for had his blade not killed the bear instantly, he and not the bear would have been the prize.

The First to Meet Ole Grizz

An even more threatening animal faced the Indian fighters out West, one far longer, heavier, and more aggressive than its "little" cousin back East. It was the grizzly bear, a roaring brown beast that often weighed eight hundred pounds and stood eight feet tall on its hind legs. Whatever the dreaded black bear could do back East, the grizzly bear could do more ferociously, whether that involved biting, clawing, slapping, or crushing its opponent to death. Many western Indian fighters eventually took on Ole Grizz but the first to do so were the members of Lewis and Clark's expedition between 1803 and 1806.

Long before they ever saw any grizzly bears, Lewis and Clark had heard outrageous tales about them from friendly Indians, tales of their size, power, and killing skills. They did not believe them, however. They thought, understandably, that the "exaggera-

Grizzly bears were tenacious enemies of frontiersmen. These mammoth animals were often able to continue fighting even after being wounded.

tions" were myths and legends. It did not take them long to discover, though, that Indian tales of the grizzly were not hyperbole and that the horrible monsters populated the West almost as prolifically as did the common beaver.

Meriwether Lewis soon wrote in his journal that, due to the ever-present grizz, "I do not think it is prudent to send one man alone on an errand of any kind."[54] But even to groups of several men, the huge bears were still a threat. One superb marksman fired a perfect shot through a rushing grizzly's heart, and still it chased him for a hundred yards, nearly bringing him down to a savage death before the bear's heart burst at last. Many mortally wounded bears managed to pursue hunters under overhanging cliffs and into rivers where the panicked men incorrectly thought that they would be safe from the behemoths.

Meriwether's Very Close Call

Lewis himself shot a grizzly and approached it, assuming that it was dead. He quickly discovered otherwise; as his journal attests:

It was on an open, level plain, not a bush within miles nor a tree within less than 300 yards. The river bank was sloping. In

When the Food Ran Low

Joe Meek once said of his starving times, "I have held my hands in an ant-hill until they were covered with ants, then greedily licked them off. I have taken the soles off my moccasins, crisped them in the fire, and eaten them."

When another man reported in dismay to Jim Bridger that he had been forced to consume the guts of a buffalo he found dead on the plains, Bridger comforted him, saying, "Don't worry. I've eaten that kind of stuff too, when I had to."

Hunger was only one of several hardships that befell Zenas Leonard on an expedition. He wrote, "Here we were in the desolate wilderness uninhabited by even the hardy savage or wild beast—surrounded on either side by huge mountains of snow, without one mouthful to eat save a few beaverskins—our eyes almost destroyed by the piercing wind, and our bodies at times almost buried by the flakes of snow which were driven before it. Oh! How heartily I wished myself home."

Thirst, hunger's evil twin, was always a problem. Various Indian fighters resorted to slashing the mules' ears to drink their blood and drinking the blood of animals that died in the desert. One even reported that the animal blood was mixed with water and boiled to make a soup.

The most outrageous example of the extremes to which a starving Indian fighter would go to sate his appetite involved one of the master trappers, Old Bill Williams. It was rumored at the Ronnyvoo that he had actually killed a man just to eat his flesh. Not many men would trap with him after that, and that was the way Old Bill liked it.

short, there was no place by means of which I could conceal myself from this monster. He pitched at me, open-mouthed, and at full speed. I ran about 80 yards and found he gained on me fast. I then ran into the water. The idea struck me to get into the water to such a depth that I could stand and he would be obliged to swim, and that I could defend myself with my espontoon (a spear-pointed weapon). The moment I put myself in this attitude of defense, he suddenly wheeled about and declined to combat.[55]

Lewis was a lucky man. Not all grizzlies gave up so readily, even when pierced by a bullet.

The Lewis and Clark expedition ultimately killed dozens of the grizzled (silver-streaked) trophies and returned to the "civilized" United States with their hides as proof that the fabled animals did, in fact, exist. Unfortunately for many Indian fighters who followed, they left enough alive for Ole Grizz to remain a common danger in the West for another hundred years.

An Eye for an Eye

Jumping into the river did not help one French-Canadian Indian fighter named Marie who had taken refuge there after wounding and riling a grizzly. The bear jumped into the water beside him and attempted to crush him in a deadly embrace. With giant paws thrashing and whitewater splashing, Marie tried diving underwater and making his escape downriver on long-held breaths of air. The ploy did not work, though. Wherever he surfaced to gasp another lungful, the dog-paddling grizzly appeared.

The Indian fighter kept up the struggle to evade his pursuer, diving and diving again. However, the pursuit ended when he came up for the last time right into the open jaws of the animal. He felt his entire head being jerked up into its mouth. The bear bit down hard, plunging one knife-edged tooth completely through his right jawbone and another deep into his right eye.

With the hole in his jaw leaking blood and water, he went limp and allowed the bear to drag him onto shore. There, Marie's partners arrived in time to shoot several ounces of fiery lead into the brute, dropping it dead with a thud. Amazingly, the Indian fighter was still alive, and his mates got him to a fort in time for badly needed medical attention. One of them later said, "I saw him six days afterward with a swelling on his head an inch thick, and his food and drink gushed through the opening under his jaw made by the teeth of his terrible enemy."[56] One can imagine what the ragged socket of his eye looked like.

One for the Indian Fighters

John Gray was a remarkable Indian fighter who was himself half Indian. He claimed Iroquois ancestry, from well east of the Mississippi, and seemed to have no qualms about killing the Indians out West, nor regarding face-to-face warfare against grizzly bears that happened by him. According to one who knew him, "He showed extraordinary courage and dexterity, especially when on one occasion he dared to attack five bears at once."[57]

Gray did not actually initiate the conflict. Not even a man as confident in his abilities as

he was would have willingly engaged five of the creatures simultaneously. He came upon one and shot it dead with his first rifle round and had time enough to reload before three more appeared. Excellent marksman that he was, he killed the boldest and largest of the three and fell back to assess his chances against the remaining two smaller, but still formidable, beasts.

Before he could load again, however, that pair burst through the bushes and rose up in roaring intimidation. But John Gray did not intimidate easily. He produced a flintlock pistol from his belt and took out the standing bear on the right with a point-blank blast through its chest. He pulled out a second pistol and brought the other animal crashing down as it charged. Surely, he thought, there could be no others so he paused to catch his breath before reloading any of his firearms. However, a fifth smaller bear attacked him from the foliage, and Gray had to meet it with a swinging rifle butt.

This bear proved more savage than the rest. He had to beat it repeatedly with his rifle-turned-club. He managed to keep it at bay, but it was clearly of a more persistent disposition than the others. Finally, as he weakened from the marathon bout, he saw an opportunity and he seized it. Flashing his long knife, he sunk it into the bear while punching its jaws away with his rifle. He stabbed it over and over until it collapsed. The other Indian fighters in his party, having heard the gunshots, rushed to his aid, but what they found was John Gray "in a circle of bears finishing off the last."[58]

Gray told and retold his story around many campfires, most likely expanding on it with each retelling. Perhaps no one will really know what happened that day other than the fact that his friends did find five dead bears around him. No doubt, the Indian fighters who listened forgave him, anyway, for any inflation of the details. For one thing, lying was expected among the rowdy frontiersmen; for another, they too could entertain the prospect of tangling with a grizzly bear (and maybe even five) and living to tell tall tales about it.

One for the Bears . . . Sort of

Jedediah Smith also lived to tell about his bear encounter, though just barely. It happened while he was leading a trapping party through the Black Hills area in 1823. The horses were suffering from the heat, dust, and prickly pear cactus on the arid plains leading up into the mountains. The men were suffering, too, as evidenced by the fact that one of them had already dehydrated along the way and had had to be buried up to his neck to absorb moisture from the deeper soil.

It was the horses' plight, however, that had caused Smith to order his men to dismount and walk their animals through a thicket of trees and bushes about a mile from a badly needed river. The shade of the foliage cooled them off a bit, as unbeknownst to them, it was doing for a sleeping grizzly bear. Jarred awake, the bear lunged down an embankment into the middle of the pack train and angrily rushed to the front of the line. Jed Smith heard the roar coming, but he could not

Three frontiersmen corner and attempt to lasso a grizzly. Most trappers and frontiersmen tried to avoid such close encounters.

Surviving the Desert: How Those Who Did, Did

Indian fighters attempting to cross a desert drank fluids regularly and avoided alcohol, which caused dehydration. They watched for the symptoms of heat stroke—cold, clammy skin, mental confusion, and loss of consciousness—and treated it by getting the victim out of the direct sun.

There were several poisonous insects of which desert travelers had to be wary. A sting from a two-inch-long scorpion was very painful and sometimes made breathing difficult. A bite from a black widow caused nausea, vomiting, and headache. The stings of bees and wasps and biting ants were also dangerous, creating welts, itching, nausea, headache, and the same difficulty in breathing. All of these insect stings or bites were treated with soap and water, damp compresses, and elevation of the bitten area. However, the Indian fighters always tried to avoid them in the first place by never putting their hands or feet in unexposed places, shaking out their clothes and shoes before putting them on, never going barefooted, and wearing no perfumes or bright clothes.

Frontiersmen dealt with rattlesnakes and poisonous Gila monsters in much the same way as they did insects, trying to avoid putting their hands and feet where they could not see. If a rattlesnake did bite, they cut open the wound with a knife, sucked out as much of the venom as they could, and let it bleed to cleanse the wound. Gila monsters, which bit and held on, had to be burned under the chin with a flame or submerged in water to force them to release their toxic jaws. Indian fighters flushed the wound with water and also let it bleed.

These are but a few of the dangers that awaited Indian fighters in the desert. It makes one pause to consider how many unknown hardships befell those who did not make it back to report them.

---

bring his rifle in time to do anything about it. According to a trapper who saw it happen, "The grizzly did not hesitate a moment but sprang upon the captain."[59]

Before anyone could help Smith, the mammoth beast jammed Smith's entire head between its jagged jaws and shook the Indian fighter violently back and forth. It finally threw his rag-doll body to the ground with a shuddering crash. Then, scooping him up in a literal bear hug, it squeezed his ribs to the point of cracking. It slashed Smith's belly open with four wounds and broke the man's long knife off at the hilt.

By then, the other trappers had recovered enough from their shock to begin pouring a heavy fire into the bear. The grizz squalled and staggered but it refused to let go of its catch. The more they shot it, the more it snarled back in defiance. After at least fifteen rounds, the bear did collapse but it still did not release Smith. He did not tumble free even when the animal jerked and spasmed with several more gunshot wounds.

No 9-1-1 to Call

No one dared venture forth to end the struggle with a knife through its heart and pry his captain away from the animal. No one had ever seen a creature with this much strength or fight. Only when it gave up its final breath, low, long, and loud, did its massive arms fall

Desert Sands, Heat, and Thirst

As of 1841, Joseph Walker had led a party of Indian fighters across the deserts of Utah and Nevada to California and returned them to the Rockies without losing a man. Earlier, Jedediah Smith had traversed those areas as well as New Mexico and Arizona but at a terrible cost in his frontiersmen's lives. John Bidwell led the third group, guided by eight seasoned Indian fighters. Miraculously, they suffered no deaths on their journey, although the unforgiving desert did its best to bring down a few of them in its searing, cotton-mouthed way. Irving Stone quotes Bidwell in *Men to Match My Mountains*:

> Started early, hoping soon to find fresh water, where we could refresh ourselves and our animals, but alas! The sun beamed heavy on our heads as the day advanced, and we could see nothing before us but extensive arid plains, glimmering with heat and salt; at length the plains became so impregnated with salt that vegetation entirely ceased; the ground was in many places white as snow with salt and perfectly smooth— the midday sun made us fancy we could see timber [and thus water] upon the plains. We marched forward with unremitted pace till we discovered it was an illusion.

The desert teased them with those titillating mirages for hundreds more miles but it provided a couple of tangible realities as well: There was little wildlife to eat and less water to drink. If they were going to survive, Bidwell and the guides knew they were going to have to improvise. And that is what they did.

They ate their horses, mules, and a scrawny wolf, including its wet eyes. They ate rattlesnakes, lizards, and acorns traded at exorbitant "prices" to primitive Indians who passed them along the way. From whatever they killed, they sucked the blood and whatever other body fluids they could keep down. Bidwell declared, "If I ever get back to Missouri, I would gladly eat out of the trough with my pigs." He never got around to dining with his livestock, though it is probable that he meant exactly what he said at the time. Indian fighters, however, pulled him and the rest of the party through to the "promised land" of California where he became one of the first U.S. citizens to take up residence there.

loose. And only then did Jedediah Smith roll limply to freedom, far nearer death than life.

Blood poured from his head and stomach; his scalp and left ear were nearly torn off. His muscled belly bore four deep gashes as if sabers, not claws, had slashed them open. His ear was "torn from his head out to the outer rim,"[60] the witness said, and his scalp was flapping over revealing the white bone of his skull. A horrendous cut ran from his left eyebrow all the way around to the back of his head. Never having treated wounds as serious as this, the other Indian fighters stood around, unsure of what to do. Jed Smith, though, shook his thoughts clear and ordered them to take a sewing needle and thread and begin stitching him up, and to preferably do so before he bled to death. Smith winced and grimaced as one of the coarse-fingered mountain men sewed his belly wounds shut and interwove his scalp flap with the rest of his face and blood-matted head. When he tried to convince Smith that he could not save his ear as it was swinging by a thin strand of flesh, Smith snarled at him to sew it on. The man reported, "I then put in my needle, stitching it through and through and over and over."[61]

Jedediah Smith lived, scarred and misshapen. He continued on with this expedition just ten days later. However, he had a whole new respect for the grizzlies now and his men had a whole new respect for him.

Staring Down the Fear

As Indian fighters gained more experience and knowledge regarding the best ways to handle grizzly bears, they discovered that one method proved more successful than all the others. It was an extremely difficult tactic to employ, though, and only men with the steadiest of nerves ever dared try it. Trapper and Indian fighter Zenas Leonard described it in his journal this way:

> The grizzly bear is the most ferocious animal that inhabits these prairies, and are very numerous. They no sooner see you than they will make at you with open mouth. If you stand still they will come to within two or three yards of you, and stand upon their hind feet and look you in the face, if you have fortitude enough to face them, they will turn and run off; but if you turn they will most assuredly tear you to pieces.[62]

Leonard and a friend had their chance to face down a grizzly but they did not take

A grizzly bear surprises a frontiersman. The animals had no fear of humans and would often attack them as they would any other prey.

Leonard's own advice, at least not completely. A huge bear burst out of a stand of bushes as they walked and raised up on its back legs in front of them as was common. The shock was too much for the two men, though, and they ran back to a tree against which their rifles were propped. The bear roared after them, teeth and claws flashing.

Their rifles proved useless, however, for they could not get either of them to fire. At that point, the last ditch, they finally stood up to Ole Grizz, beating it about the face and head with their rifle butts. Probably due more to luck than Leonard's theory about facing bears, the creature retreated and went its own way, leaving Leonard to wonder if he would ever be able to employ his tactic at the beginning of a bear encounter.

One Indian fighter who was able to do so was Tom "Old Broken Hand" Fitzpatrick. A grizzly attacked him running as fast as a bear can run. Since he was on foot, Fitzpatrick planted both of them and stood the attacker down. On cue, the bear began to backpedal and slid on its rump to a complete stop just two yards away from Fitzpatrick. The angry-eyed man and eight-hundred-pound bear stared each other squarely in the eyes. Downplaying what surely must have been a moment of extreme inner panic, Fitzpatrick later

The Indian Fighter's Guide to Survival in the Snow

Indian fighters knew that a positive attitude was central to winter survival. To survive when trapped in the snow, they had to fill every waking moment with thoughts that they would make it, that they could persevere. Then they could attempt to overcome their next two challenges: exposure and dehydration.

The key to beating exposure was building a fire, and to do that they had to provide a windless shelter. The shelter did not take long to build. It was, in fact, just a mound of packed snow out of which they dug a little cave. Once inside, they would snip off a dry piece of woolen clothing and use it as kindling. They then proceeded to add progressively bigger twigs and branches (found dry under logs). They did not bother with pine cones or bark, which they knew did not burn.

Experienced frontiersmen kept a lookout for frostbite, the freezing of fingers, toes, ears, and nose. The first sign was the extremity turning white, then tingling, numbing, and turning black. Rewarming the affected areas was the only antidote. Hypothermia, the lowering of the body temperature, caused uncontrollable shivering, memory loss, disorientation, slurred speech, exhaustion, and death. Once again, heat and shelter provided the only hope of survival.

Dehydration, which caused a steady descent from fatigue into death, provided the second serious challenge to the Indian fighters for, in the winter, they never felt thirsty even when their fluid levels were way down. So regardless of whether they wanted a drink of water or not, they knew they had to keep pouring it down in large amounts. Eating snow did not help because that further reduced their body temperature, as did drinking alcohol. Instead, they first melted the snow into water over the fire and then drank as much as they could make.

Once they had secured warmth and water, they could then start their search for food.

reported, "Then after discovering that I was in no ways bashful, it bowed, turned and ran—and I did the same, and made for my horse."[63]

Revealing Fear

Few men, however, were able to employ the technique that Zenas Leonard wrote about and "Old Broken Hand" Fitzpatrick mastered. And no one ever called them cowards because they could not. Most Indian fighters were brave men with a normal reaction to fearsome beasts and the near-death experiences they created. Indian fighter and trapper Osbourne Russell related in his journal his close call with a grizzly bear. It occurred while he and his partners were treading along some bushes:

> We heard a sudden growl which was instantly followed by the spring of a grizzly bear toward us; his enormous jaws extended and eyes flashing fire. Was ever anything so hideous? We could not retain sufficient presence of mind to shoot at him but took to our heels separating as we ran, the bear taking after me. I was obliged to turn about and face him. I pulled the trigger and knew not what else to do and hardly knew that I did this but it accidentally happened that my rifle was pointed towards the bear when I pulled and the ball piercing his heart, he uttered a deathly howl and fell dead: but I trembled as if I had an ague [fever] fit for half an hour after.[64]

The fact that such a normally boastful frontiersman would openly and honestly reveal the frazzling terror he experienced when facing a grizzly bear gives further evidence to the fearful sway the animals held over the men. Apparently, it was acceptable to admit a fear of grizzlies but not of the equally deadly Indians.

Indian-fighting legend Kit Carson rarely admitted to his fears and, judging by his exploits, it is likely that he did not have many. When it came to fighting the grizz, though, Carson took his already considerable humility several steps further. While out hunting one very nearly fatal afternoon, not one but two of the agitated bears attacked him from behind. Carson reported:

> My gun was unloaded and I could not possibly reload in time to fire. There were some trees at a short distance. I made for them, the bears after me. As I got to one of the trees, I had to drop my gun—the bear rushing for me, I had to make all haste to ascend the tree. I got up some ten or fifteen feet and then had to remain until the bears would find it convenient to leave. I was never so scared in my life.[65]

No doubt, he was never so hungry either, for the bears kept him treed that way until well after it was too dark to hunt down a meal.

A Man Named Meek Who Was Anything But

Perhaps the happiest, smilingest lover of good times on the frontier was Joe Meek, a bald, bearded, roly-poly Santa Claus of a man with sparkling eyes, cherubic cheeks, and a joke for every occasion. It seems a bit odd that such a rotund and elfin Indian fighter could have waged war with the grizzlies but that is exactly what he did, to the point of going out and looking for them and their majestic furs.

According to historical record, frontiersman Joe Meek was extremely personable and cheerful for an Indian fighter.

One incident that Joe Meek reported occurred when he and another trapper spotted a grizzly on the far side of a cold, rapid stream. They each shot the animal and assumed that they had killed it so they stripped down to nothing but their knife and hatchet belt for the brisk swim over to their trophy. As often happened when attempting to kill an animal as large and rugged as a grizzly, the furry prize turned out to be only wounded, and it leaped up after them and chased them back to the stream. Meek said later, "The bank was about fifteen feet above the water and the river ten or twelve feet deep; but we didn't halt. Overboard we went, the bear after us."[66]

With the paddling grizzly right behind them, the two naked men burst out of the water and blazed a sodden trail to their mounts, reaching them in time to grab their clothes but not to put them on. They kicked the normally stubborn mules hard in the flanks but the animals were already spooking at the sound of the approaching roar and off the two Indian fighters rode. Meek was already laughing uncontrollably when they made it back to the camp, and the men there lost no time in joining in. Only Joe Meek, they said, "could go off looking for a bear's cover and wind up losing his own."[67] And Joe Meek, true to form, took the ribbing well while, of course, dressing himself as rapidly as possible.

Laughter, however, over close calls with bears or anything else became a faded echo for any man, white or Indian, anticipating or remembering the horror of full-scale war. Rare as it might have been on the frontier, its tentacles clung the longest within the entwined nightmares of those who survived it.

The Great Battles

Indians usually preferred to engage their enemies individually or in small groups. Whenever soldiers or frontiersmen gathered in numbers over five hundred, they would wait to attack until smaller squads broke away and made themselves more vulnerable targets. That was a most effective strategy, because small-unit skirmishes best suited the fiercely individualistic fighting style of warriors who were notorious for refusing to obey commands in the heat of battle. Most chiefs had long since decided that it was easier to manage ten or twelve blood-blinded braves running helter-skelter than a thousand of them. Besides, the great majority of warlike tribes hated each other so infernally as to render impossible the alliances that large-unit warfare would have required.

There were notable exceptions, however. Sometimes large numbers of Indian warriors would bond together to take on an equal-size army of white men, especially when the whites foolishly lined up like toy soldiers out in the open to do their regimentalized fighting. In fact, such early successes as the defeat of General Braddock's British regulars near Fort Duquesne (present-day Pittsburgh) in 1754 deceived the Indians into thinking that all whites could be easily beaten. What they did not count on was the buckskin Indian fighters learning their ways and forming armies of their own, eventually fighting the way they did and just as well.

Armies in the Forest

The frontiersmen of early Virginia were the first to wage a full-scale battle against the Shawnee Indians at the Battle of Point Pleasant during Lord Dunsmore's War in 1774. Dunsmore was the governor of Virginia at the time, and he wanted to clear western Virginia of Indians so that settlers could take over the land. The battle would be regarded by some as the first of the Revolutionary War in that it secured the Virginia frontier so that her sons could go off to fight the British.

On October 10, 1774, approximately one thousand half-clad, painted Indians crept catlike through the forest near the junction of the Kanawha and Ohio Rivers. They carried flintlocks, tomahawks, knives, and spiked war clubs. Some had rapid-fire bows and skin-slitting arrows. The boys showed fear on their illustrated faces; the men showed only ferocity. About a thousand hidden Indian fighters were waiting for them.

First Contact

Rifles sounded somewhere in the near distance. Nervous eyes flashed to the flanks. War whoops lanced the leaves of the trees and swelled to a skin-tingling din. Hearts beat faster. Mouths went dry. And then it happened. Hellfire and the devil's own

A frontiersman takes aim at Indian attackers during the Revolutionary War.

damnation broke loose in the darkened gloom. In seconds, two thousand flintlocks touched off with shuddering booms and quick-popping pa-thacks. Each man on either side took to a tree and clutched the scant cover it offered. Swirling blue smoke rushed forth from both armies and mingled within the primeval green. A sun shaft here and there made a filtered beam that no one noticed.

Bullets sucked air, chipped wood, and kicked up dirt. Dead leaves scattered on the moist, mulched earth. Men reloaded and fired, fired and reloaded. Both forces disintegrated into small groups and then lone warriors. The bullets flew, the smoke grew, and the rot of sulfur and wet earth wafted into nostrils already blackened by gunpowder.

Toward a Climax

Isaac Shelby, one of the white Indian fighters, understated the horror, saying only, "It was a very hard day; sometimes the hideous cries of the enemy, and the groans of our wounded men lying around was enough to shudder the stoutest heart. The action continued hot all day and the bravest of their men made good use of themselves."[68]

Indeed, they did. When dusk finally descended and the survivors on both sides limped away dazed, the Shawnee left behind 40 men dead among the trees, while the Indian fighters gathered up 75 of their own with another 140 wounded. It was the Indians, however, who decided to retreat during the night, leaving the smoldering forest and the victory to the frontiersmen. More importantly, the Shawnee leaders decided that, since the whites could now obviously fight as well as they could in the wilderness, they should make peace with them and the hordes sure to follow. It was that peace that calmed the Virginia frontier and allowed the backwoods boys to go fight the British for their independence.

A Shameful Foray into Total War

By 1779, three of the five tribes of the Iroquois Nation in upper New York had allied themselves with the British against the Americans in the Revolutionary War. The other two tribes attempted to remain neutral. Due to the masterful fighting abilities of the Iroquois braves and the resulting setbacks they were causing the American troops throughout the Iroquois homelands, General George Washington issued the following order to Major General John Sullivan, who commanded regular troops and a large number of Indian fighters: "Attack the Iroquois and lay waste all the settlements around that the country may not be merely overrun but destroyed. Do not listen to any overture of peace before the total ruin of their settlements is effected."[69]

The resulting conflagration consumed not only the homes, cultivated fields, orchards, and hunting grounds of the Iroquois tribes fighting against them but also of those who had not sent braves against them. Men, women, children, and livestock felt the mighty rush of American vengeance until the land had been so scourged as to make it uninhabitable. The survivors fled to Canada, leaving behind bodies that had been flayed by some of the soldiers and frontiersmen to make boot tops and leggings.

Afterward, Washington's general wrote back to him that he had, "destroyed everything that contributes to the Iroquois' support and turned the whole garden scene to one of dreary and sickening desolation. The Indians were hunted like wild beasts in a war of

An American soldier sets fire to an Indian village as a woman and her children flee. During the Revolutionary War, George Washington ordered the villages destroyed.

extermination."[70] The Americans forced a treaty out of the Iroquois, but they did not always have their way with the Indian, however, as many found out farther south.

Laying a Trap

Down in Kentucky, the killing was a little more balanced. The Ohio Indians had never signed a peace treaty with the Indian fighters. Nor were they likely to while British officers like Henry Hamilton, the "Hair Buyer," and white-man-turned-Indian Simon Girty agitated the Indians against the Americans. Hamilton worked from his plush headquarters in Detroit by paying Indians for the scalps of whites. Girty got more closely involved, personally leading Indian war parties against the people he had once called his own.

In 1782 Girty led a band of some five hundred Ohio Indians across the Ohio River to attack white settlements in Kentucky. He had his sights set on Bryan's Station, not far from Boonesborough, but he failed to attack before the settlers had gathered in their people and closed the gate.

Aware that he had squandered an opportunity and angered his Indian friends, Girty wanted a fight more than ever. He devised a

Crack Shots for Andy

When Andrew Jackson headed south to take command of the Americans guarding New Orleans during the War of 1812, he made certain that as many Indian fighters in buckskin as possible came along. As an old Tennessee Indian fighter himself, he knew the value of these raucous, hard-drinking illiterates.

The night before the battle, Jackson sent a contingent of Tennessee frontiersmen out in "hunting parties" to quietly stalk and cut the throats of British sentries. When he needed sharpshooters to keep the heads of the Britishers down and thereby mask the movement of his artillery, he once again called on the long riflemen from Tennessee and Kentucky.

Jackson eagerly anticipated the arrival during the night of twenty-three hundred Kentuckians, who, he assumed, were all crack Indian fighters. It turned out, to his disappointment, that only seven hundred of them were bona fide frontiersmen. The rest were merely farmers who had responded to the call for volunteers, many of whom did not even have rifles. He scraped up some small bird-hunting guns (fowling pieces) for them and they ended up doing considerable damage to the enemy. Their initial lack of arms, however, prompted Jackson's comment, recorded in H. L. Coles's *The War of 1812*, "I have never seen a Kentuckian without a gun and a pack of cards and a bottle of whiskey in my life."

The next morning, 8,000 British regulars passed by the regiment, advancing like toy soldiers toward the 5,000 Americans who were well protected in a plantation canal ditch. Along with all the other Americans, the Indian fighters picked off the exposed English soldiers by the score. The day ended with 300 of the British dead, 1,250 of them horribly maimed, and another 500 captured and imprisoned. Jackson's force lost only 14 dead, 39 wounded, and 18 captured and quickly released.

It was a monumental victory for the struggling United States of America and one over which the Indian fighters no doubt celebrated mightily.

An editorial cartoon depicts a British officer accepting American scalps from his Indian allies. British officer Henry Hamilton was well-known for paying Indians for American scalps.

trap and he executed it masterfully, having his warriors leave an obvious trail and even going so far as to "blaze" trees along the path of their "retreat." He headed the braves back toward Ohio and crossed the Licking River, but went no farther.

Falling for It

As Girty anticipated, a force of about two hundred Indian fighters led by the brash Lieutenant Colonel John Todd of the local militia set off in a blind, racing pursuit like hounds crazed with the scent of blood. Daniel Boone and his young son Israel were among the party; the elder Boone cautioned Colonel Todd to slow down and wait for the force of four hundred men that was following some-

where behind them. He pointed out many times that Girty's Indians were leaving too obvious a trail and that it could only lead them into an ambush. Upon reaching the Licking River, Boone again advised caution. He pointed out two wooded ravines on the other side that could hide all of the Indians they were after.

Colonel Todd, however, condemned Boone's timidity and yelled out to the others, "By Godly! What have we come here for? All who are not damned cowards follow me!"[71] And with the fever of impending victory boiling their brains, these brave, foolish men splashed across the river and started up the bare hill before them. Just as the first of them reached the top, the air convulsed with the shrill war cries of Girty's braves as they poured out of the ravines with guns blazing and tomahawks glinting. Some of the braves ran to the bottom of the hill and cut off the white men's retreat.

The Trap Snaps Shut

Panic fritzed the Indian fighters' nerves. They screamed like children to break free. Bullets zinged. War clubs thudded. Steel knives dripped red with their blood. The dead collapsed, the wounded stumbled, the rest turned and sprinted to the river like scalded dogs. More fell lifeless. Others tripped, stricken. Scores of Indian fighters ran for their very lives.

The shouting, the moaning, the wailing, the crying all reverberated in their ears. Their eyes burned with smoke and tears as they tumbled down the slope to the water. Vines and underbrush entangled them along the bank. Men threw down their rifles to better flee. And the harder they ran, the slower they went, their legs turning leaden and sluggish.

Another foot, another yard, another leg heaved heavily in front of the other and on they pressed to escape this hornet hive. Bullets smashed into them but they were finally back to the river, those still on their feet, and they flailed into the water like windmills until they reached the succoring forest on the other side.

Daniel Boone got caught in the middle of the river. He saw his son take a bullet to the head. He waded to him, desperate and afraid as he had never been afraid before, and he tried to lift his dying boy over his shoulder. But a brave came at him with his scalping knife, and he had to drop the boy to defend himself. All he recalled later was finding himself on the far shore without his precious son. Sensing that the wound to the boy's head was fatal and knowing also that it would be

suicide for him to return for his body, he straggled off with the rest of the ragtag retreaters, sobbing like a child.

Burying the Losers, Paying Off the Winners

Five days later, Boone returned to the scene of the Indian fighters' massacre, the Indians' magnificent victory, to recover young Israel's body. He found it onshore, bloated, black, scalped, and stinking. He could only identify it by the clothing. He would later write, "We proceeded to bury the dead which were 43 on the ground and many more we expect lay about that we did not see."[72] Daniel Boone would rarely speak of this incident again and, each time that he did, he wept.

For his part, the British colonel Hamilton paid handsomely for the many scalps taken at the Battle of Blue Licks (named for the salt lick nearby) and he was, of course, pleased with the strategic effect. It was the first larger-scale battle that his Indian allies had won against the American Indian fighters, and it encouraged them to keep on fighting. It was for Simon Girty the high point of a lifetime spent battling white Indian fighters, a stand-up battle planned well and fought bravely. It was also considered by many to be the last battle of the Revolutionary War although it would perhaps be more correctly remembered as the second battle for the Northwest Territory.

A Bodacious Plan

The first battle for the Northwest Territory (what would later become the states of Ohio, Indiana, Michigan, Wisconsin, Illinois, and part of Minnesota) had occurred a year earlier in February 1779. Colonel Hamilton, the

Hair Buyer, had failed to properly reinforce the British forts at Kaskaskia and Vincennes in southern Illinois and that had given Colonel George Rogers Clark an idea. The twenty-six-year-old Clark had been raised as a Virginia plantation gentleman, but he had long since forsaken the pleasures and amenities of the genteel life for the rugged hardships of the frontier. By 1779 he had proven himself to be as tough as any Indian fighter west of the Appalachians and a charismatic leader among them.

In July 1778 Clark raised a force of two hundred Indian fighters and led them against the British and their Indian allies at Kaskaskia and Vincennes, which he considered the stepping-stones to English-held Detroit itself. He took them both by stealthy "Indian ways," barely having to fire a shot. Before he could organize a force of frontiersmen large enough to attack Detroit, however, Hamilton marched his Indians and redcoats down to Vincennes and recaptured it for the British. This countermove enraged Clark to the point that he swore "to attack the enemy in his stronghold."[73]

Complicating his plan, February 1779 was unusually cold and heavy downpours of frigid

Daniel Boone attempts to fend off an Indian attacker to rescue his son. Boone was forced to retreat, leaving the fatally wounded boy behind.

Victory at Last at Fallen Timbers

By 1792 two large U.S. Army forces and several smaller militia groups had already failed dismally to clear the British and their Indians out of the Northwest Territory. President George Washington, enraged as only he could be at the continuous defeats, put his old friend and proven winner during the Revolutionary War in charge. He was General "Mad" Anthony Wayne and he promised the resolute president that he would succeed where all others had failed.

Contrary to the impetuous, wild-charging style that had won him so many battles during the Revolution, Wayne took two full years to raise, train, equip, and advance his army across Ohio to Detroit. He fought many small actions along the way, built extensive earthworks every night, and constructed one of the finest forts ever seen on the frontier for his winter respite. All that work paid off the following spring.

In an area of tornado-downed trees near present-day Toledo, Ohio (just south of Detroit), Wayne and his army (the flankers and sharpshooters made up of two hundred Kentucky Indian fighters) attacked the British-armed and -led force of Indians in a full-scale battle by any frontier standard. Wayne himself had twenty-one hundred disciplined soldiers at his disposal; the Indians and British brought out fifteen hundred.

According to Richard Knopf's *Anthony Wayne*, the outcome was fixed. General Wayne became his old "Mad" self again and cried out, "The standing order of the day is 'Charge the damned rascals with the bayonets!'" His men obeyed with the precision he had drilled into them. And, watching through his field glass, he rejoiced forty minutes later, "The savages with their allies are abandoning themselves to flight and dispersing with terror and dismay!"

Reflecting on the rout, he later wrote, "The woods were strewn for a considerable distance with the dead bodies of Indians and their white auxiliaries, the latter armed with British muskets and bayonets."

And so it ended at last. The British packed up and left Detroit rather than resist General Wayne's magnificent little army. The victory at Fallen Timbers also led to the signing of the Treaty of Greenville, ceding from the Indians in fact and practice most of present-day Ohio.

"Mad" Anthony Wayne was anything but mad when he systematically trained a group of soldiers to fight against the British and their Indian allies.

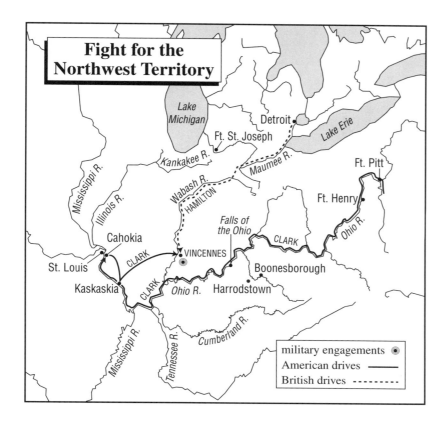

Fight for the Northwest Territory

rain and sleet had flooded every river, creek, trail, and road on his proposed attack route into one vast ice-encrusted swamp. If he was to move his Indian fighters secretly into battle, he would have to lead them first through the ankle-, waist-, and chin-deep waters stretching the entire 240 miles from his base at Kaskaskia to Fort Sackville, protecting the village of Vincennes. And that is exactly what he set out to do.

Suffering Too Incredible to Believe

From February 5 nonstop to February 29, Clark and his two hundred buckskin-clad men sloshed, tramped, splashed, waded, swam, and mucked their way forward step by

agonizing step through freezing waters, boot-sucking mud, and ice blocks that crashed into them at the speed of the racing currents. Lips quivered, hands shook, legs went numb and stung up to the crotch. Fingers turned white, toes went from blue to black, and still these coughing men struggled on.

According to Clark, "The suffering was too incredible for any person to believe . . . but we saw but one alternative, which was to attack. The men abandoned all thought of retreat, preferring to undergo any difficulty that offered a prospect of success, rather than to attempt a retreat involving the certainty of encountering all they had already endured."[74]

So on they drove, wheezing and hacking, knowing in their misery-fogged minds that each squishing, biting, nipping step they

George Rogers Clark leads his men across the flooded Wabash River and through cold and icy swamps to attack Fort Vincennes.

slogged ahead in the freezing mire made the trip back that much farther. Clark encouraged them "with the thought of the magnitude of the consequences that would attend our success. If we were successful, we would thereby save the whole American cause."[75] And just in case his little encouragements did not properly motivate his aching, throbbing men, he placed twenty-five of his most durable marksmen behind them with orders to shoot anyone who tried to drop out.

Whatever the motivation, these two hundred Indian fighters, all frozen-wet to their cores and suffering excruciating pain from frostbite, exposure, and hypothermia, somehow managed to dredge up just enough strength to make one more step, one more yard, and then one more mile, day after body-racking day. Two tortured weeks passed and the men kept staggering forward. At least, it couldn't get any worse, some among them must have muttered, but it did. Their rations ran out.

From Survivors to Warriors

At last, their stubborn, grinding willpower began to pay off. They made it to ground higher than that of the chilling waters and within striking distance of the redcoats and their red men. At that blessed point, the clammy skeletons found enough dead wood to start fires big enough to thaw themselves and dry their buckskins. Adding to their change of fortune, an Indian woman canoed by with a load of fresh buffalo meat which Clark's men quickly confiscated, cooked, and gorged themselves nearly to bursting. Clark rested his troops for the remainder of the day and then marched them, over reasonably dry land, to the village of Vincennes that night.

The Frenchmen who predominantly inhabited the little collection of log huts made no effort to resist the Americans. In fact, they had recently heard that France had come into the Revolutionary War on the American side and, hence, were now allies with the Kentucky Indian fighters. Further, they gave Clark and his men dry gunpowder to replace that which had been ruined during their icy ordeal and kept the Americans' presence a secret so that they could take the nearby fort by surprise.

The marksmen surrounded the stockade and shot down the inattentive sentries shuffling around the tops of the walls. They aimed at lights flickering through the open gun ports and wounded several more of the stunned enemy. When the British artillerists tried to man their big guns from atop the palisade, they also rapidly fell, easy targets to the backwoods sharpshooters. Hiding behind rocks and trees and rolling for new cover after each shot, the frontiersmen poured a vicious stream of bullets into the fort and suffered no casualties themselves.

Surrender and Victory

By midmorning, the fate of Henry Hamilton, the Hair Buyer, seemed clear. He and his redcoats and Indians were cut off and surrounded with no significant chance of being rescued. George Rogers Clark sent him this ominous surrender note: "Sir:—In order to save yourself from the impending storm which threatens you, I order you to immediately surrender yourself . . . for if I am obliged

to storm, you may depend upon such treatment as is justly due a murderer."[76]

Hamilton refused; for the next day the two forces skirmished off and on without result. The two commanders exchanged more notes and even met at one point face-to-face but nothing budged the standoff. On the third day of the siege, however, an Indian war party attempting to relieve the fort fell grotesquely afoul of the Indian fighters. After killing most of them in an ambush, they found four surviving braves carrying white men's scalps from Kentucky, presumably to sell to Hamilton.

It should be noted at this point that "buying and selling" the scalps of opponents on the frontier was a common practice not only among the British and their Indian allies but among the Americans themselves. Technically, both sides could argue that they were not really buying and selling the horrible trophies because they did not usually exchange money for them. Instead, the "buyer" simply

The letter Colonel Clark wrote to Henry Hamilton demanding his unconditional surrender of Fort Vincennes.

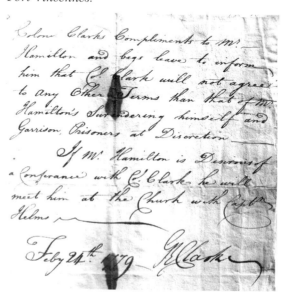

From Fame to Shame

After winning the Battle of Vincennes, George Rogers Clark was touted as one of the greatest heroes of his age. He was twenty-six years old and had every reason to look forward to a long and illustrious career in the military and, some said, in national politics as well. Almost immediately, however, his star began to lose its luster. The states of Virginia and Kentucky failed to live up to their promises to man and equip an army with which Clark would seize Detroit, still in British hands.

The fledgling U.S. government failed to pay him even for his capture of Vincennes, and his debtors began to circle like buzzards. As a matter of honor, General Clark spent his own money paying back the men who had supplied his Kaskaskia and Vincennes triumphs. Clark attempted to fight the Ohio, Indiana, and Illinois Indians, but without payments for his men and adequate supplies, he failed. The army dismissed him for those failures, and he languished as a minor government functionary for several years after that.

He spent his later life as a miserable alcoholic in a lonely log cabin overlooking the Ohio River at Louisville, Kentucky. He tried hard but could not enjoy his younger brother's unprecedented fame and success as co-commander of the Lewis and Clark expedition. The elder Clark died in 1818, broke and broken. It would take two centuries, but a monument would finally be erected in his honor at Vincennes, Indiana, the site of his forgotten greatness.

George Rogers Clark was promptly forgotten by the U.S. government after his victory at the Battle of Vincennes.

wanted to reward the efficient service of his men and "gave" them rifles, tomahawks, food, and other supplies.

Scalps remained an important prize on both sides of the Indian wars, however, as evidenced by the words of one of the most ardent Indian haters ever to fight them: President Andrew Jackson. He once boasted, "I have on all occasions preserved the scalps of my killed . . . the savage dogs."[77]

Regardless of the fact that scalp-taking was an accepted practice among both whites and Indians, George Rogers Clark was outraged and frustrated by the sight of this latest batch. He brashly ordered the four bound captives hauled out in plain view of the fort and brutally tomahawked to death as retribution and as a clear warning of what he intended to do to the people inside the stockade if they did not surrender. After blustering some outrage and frustration of his own, Hamilton gave up the fight, thereby submitting himself to three years of chains, shackles, and ridicule in a dank Williamsburg, Virginia, dungeon.

George Rogers Clark and his men became national heroes, having laid the groundwork for Great Britain's eventual expulsion from the American-claimed Northwest Territory. It would take a few more years and a few more battles to cement the claim to this essential region and, in the future, organized and uniformed armies would do most of the fighting. The influence of the Indian fighters on large, set-piece battles would be long felt, however. U.S. Army troops would fight Indians "Indian style" more and more and traditionally trained army officers would take Indian fighters into battle with them to serve as scouts, spies, sharpshooters, translators, hunters, and commando-style rangers. Warfare would never be the same.

The Horrible Truth

In recent years, many historians and social critics have condemned the United States for its removal of the American Indians from their land and for the manner in which it did so. No doubt, the atrocities, broken treaties, and massacres that have been brought to light did occur and did hasten the demise of the native cultures, but most of the European-Americans' gains were due to fairly fought, face-to-face battles noted for the courage and fighting skills displayed by warriors on both sides.

It is important, nonetheless, to place the deeds of the white Americans in the broader context of world history. While that context does not and should not exonerate the United States from its harshness when taking the Indians' lands, a review of human migration and empire building throughout the ages tends to place the western migration of American pioneers and Indian fighters in a clearer perspective.

The Nature of the Human Beast

Simply put, the stronger, more populous, and technologically superior cultures have been invading and taking the lands of their weaker neighbors since the dawn of man. From Egypt to Persia to the Greeks and Romans expansionist butchery has prevailed. One ancient Chinese dynasty after another, the Han, Sui, Tang, and Ming, brutally overtook the one preceding it in the name of empire or divine right, and the Mongol, Byzantine, and Muslim cultures all claimed foreign territory and foreign riches through ruthless conquest.

In black Africa, the successive empires of Ghana, Mali, Zimbabwe, and the Congo rose to greatness on the bloodied backs of other less developed blacks while the Ottoman Turks descended in savage hordes on the unfortunate peoples of the north. Asians by the thousands lost their heads to Japanese samurai, and the Catholic Holy Roman Empire was no less brutal when it sent Charlemagne to mangle the northern Europeans. The Olmecs, Mayans, Incas, and Aztecs of early America made their civilizations great by torturing, enslaving, and sacrificing their beaten enemies until Spanish, French, and English armies eventually did the same to them.

And the American Indians constantly warred with their neighbors for rights to hunting grounds, resources, and living space. Centuries before a single white man appeared on American soil, they were raiding, torturing, murdering, raping, enslaving, and otherwise persecuting their red-skinned "brothers."

It was against this backdrop of unending human conflict that the Indian fighters took to the woods. Most were poor people whose families had been denied land and freedom in their European countries of origin and had been driven from their homes in one fashion or another. And homes were what they hoped to find here by pushing the Indians farther and farther west. They were men, these Indian fighters, like men throughout the ages who dreamed of something better for themselves and their families; men who were aggressive and determined enough to take it from whomever happened to have it at the time.

Historical Trends: Easier Read than Done

And taking it was not easy for them. The Indian fighters constantly faced a ruthless and brave opponent who at first got the best of them in battle. The odds for their survival speak for themselves. In one year, 116 frontiersmen left Santa Fe and only 16 made it back alive. Of 300 men whom one graying Indian fighter had known in his career, only 3 survived with him to age 60. All others had died some form of violent death—combat, disease, bears, wolves, snakebite, starvation, dehydration, freezing, drowning, lack of medicine, broken bones, and firearm accidents to name but a few.

The body count was a long one. Jedediah Smith lost a rifle fight with Comanches in the southwestern desert at the age of thirty-two. Daniel Boone's son Israel died much younger at the hands of Simon Girty's Shawnee. At twenty-six, West Virginia Indian fighter Jacob Reger disappeared on a long scout, presumably a victim of the Delaware, and another Boone boy found himself tied to a torturing post, slowly burning to death. Meriwether Lewis returned from the Lewis and Clark expedition a hero only to commit suicide three

Two men anxiously peer into the dense woods, on the lookout for an Indian ambush. Life on the frontier was hard and often short.

years later with the same two pistols that had helped open the Louisiana Territory. Zebulon Pike advanced through the army ranks only to be killed leading his men against the British during the War of 1812. And as every American schoolchild knows, David "Davy" Crockett ended his fifty years of life at the legendary Battle of the Alamo.

The Chosen Few

Even more remarkable than the high number of early deaths among the Indian fighters as they endeavored to separate the natives from their lands is the number of them who somehow managed to survive into old age. Due to luck, fate, God's will, or their own skill, many (still a marked minority) lived to write books or become the subjects of them and, therefore, be remembered yet today.

William Clark, for example, Meriwether Lewis's partner, lived happily to full maturity, serving as the U.S. superintendent of Indian Affairs. After fighting large bands of Indians as a Union general during the Civil War, Kit Carson passed on from natural causes at the age of fifty-eight. Jim Bridger met every one of his life-threatening challenges to survive until age seventy-seven on a peaceful farm in Missouri. Joe Walker hit seventy-eight on a California farm before passing into the backwaters of history. Joe Meek, the Happy Mountain Man, mellowed into his later years as a U.S. marshal in the Oregon Territory.

An Old Man Rocking on a Porch

Of all the Indian fighters who survived to rock their grandchildren to sleep, none will ever surpass the revered status in the American psyche held by Daniel Boone. He retired to the Missouri farm of his middle-aged daughter Jemima, whom he had rescued from her Indian captors when she was just a girl. He had lost all his money but paid all his debts, even to the lawyers who had cheated him of his once-vast landholdings. But he did not hold grudges. He was a laughing old man and he cherished the memories of his storied life.

He also cherished the idea that he had seen so much history transpire in his eighty-five years and taken part in a great deal of it: the French and Indian War, the settling of Pennsylvania, North Carolina, Tennessee, and, especially, Kentucky. He saw the Revolutionary War forge thirteen British colonies into the United States of America and watched it grow to the Mississippi. Now, Jemima read him all the reports about Lewis and Clark, Zebulon Pike, John Colter, and the first whites to penetrate the Far West and they caused his emotions to mix.

He knew the rest of the American continent would eventually fall to the Indian fighters and it saddened him to think that the Indians whom he had always respected would fall with it. However, it stirred his heart when trappers, huntsmen, soldiers, and frontiersmen of every ilk stopped by his farm and told him their tales about that fabled western wilderness. A land of new adventures, untrammeled lands, and great men, both Indian and white, with whom to share them. Had he lived a few more years, he would have certainly shared his porch with men like Jedediah Smith, Jim Bridger, Tom Fitzpatrick, and Joseph Walker; and perhaps even Joe Meek, Kit Carson, Isaac Shelby, and John C. Fremont later on.

But even without knowing who the next generation of Indian fighters would be, he knew what they would be. They would be like James Smith, David Crockett, Squire Boone, Jesse Hughes, Lewis Wetzel, Jacob Reger,

Daniel Boone survived his wilderness adventures to retire to his daughter's farm and live to old age.

Ebenezer Zane, and himself. They would be men willing to kill Indians to save their friends, drive Indian families from their lands to make homesteads for their own families, and destroy the loved ones of others in order to insure the security of their own. Surely, old Daniel Boone must have known that they would be complex and contradictory men, possessing equal parts of love and hate, gentleness and ferocity, sensitivity and hard-hearted callousness. They would be Indian fighters like those who had gone before them. And for better or for worse, they would lead America into the future.

Notes

Introduction: Boone: The Exemplar

1. Quoted in John Filson, *The Discovery, Settlement, and Present State of Kentucke.* New York: Corinth Books, 1962.

2. Quoted in Filson, *Discovery.*

3. Quoted in Filson, *Discovery.*

4. Quoted in John Bakeless, *Daniel Boone.* New York: Stackpole, 1965.

Chapter 1: Furs and Fortunes: The First Grounds for Conflict

5. Quoted in Robert Cleland, *This Reckless Breed of Men.* New York: Knopf, 1952.

6. Quoted in Albert N. Josephy Jr., *500 Nations.* New York: Knopf, 1994.

7. Arrel Morgan Gibson, *The American Indian.* Lexington, MA: D. C. Heath, 1980.

8. Quoted in Gibson, *The American Indian.*

9. Quoted in John C. Ewers, ed., *The Adventures of Zenas Leonard—Fur Trader.* Norman: University of Oklahoma Press, 1959.

10. Quoted in Ewers, *The Adventures of Zenas Leonard.*

11. Quoted in Grace C. Nute, *The Voyageurs.* St. Paul: Minnesota Historical Society, 1989.

12. Jedediah Smith, *The Southwest Expeditions of Jedediah Smith.* Lincoln: University of Nebraska Press, 1989.

Chapter 2: Trailblazers in the East

13. Quoted in Thomas Froncek, ed., *Voices from the Wilderness.* New York: McGraw-Hill, 1974.

14. Bakeless, *Daniel Boone.*

15. Quoted in William T. Hagan, *American Indians.* Chicago: University of Chicago Press, 1961.

16. Zanesville Ohio Web Page. Microsoft Internet Explorer, 1996.

17. Edward Tunis, *Frontier Living.* New York: World Publishing, 1961.

18. Tunis, *Frontier Living.*

Chapter 3: Pathfinding West of the Mississippi

19. Bernard DeVoto, ed., *The Journals of Lewis and Clark.* New York: Houghton-Mifflin, 1953.

20. DeVoto, *Journals.*

21. DeVoto, *Journals.*

22. DeVoto, *Journals.*

23. Quoted in Jared Stallones, *Zebulon Pike.* New York: Chelsea, 1976.

24. DeVoto, *Journals.*

25. Quoted in Cleland, *The Reckless Breed of Men.*

26. Quoted in Cleland, *The Reckless Breed of Men.*

27. Smith, *The Southwest Expeditions.*

28. Quoted in Harold Melton, *Jim Beckwourth, Negro Mountain Man.* New York: Dodd, Mead, 1970.

29. Quoted in Melton, *Jim Beckwourth.*

30. Quoted in Melton, *Jim Beckwourth.*

31. Quoted in Cecil Alter, *James Bridger.* New York: Shepard, 1955.

32. Quoted in Alter, *James Bridger.*

33. Quoted in Alter, *James Bridger*.

34. Quoted in Allan Nevins, *Fremont: Pathmarker of the West*. New York: Frederick, 1961.

Chapter 4: Skirmishes and Single Warrior Combat in the East

35. Quoted in Bakeless, *Daniel Boone*.

36. David E. Stannard, *American Holocaust*. New York: Oxford University Press, 1992.

37. Quoted in J. DeHass, *History of the Early Settlement and Indian Wars of West Virginia*. Parsons, WV: McClain, 1990.

38. Quoted in DeHass, *History*.

Chapter 5: Face to Face in the West

39. Hiram M. Chittendon, *The American Fur Trade of the Far West*. New York: F. P. Harper, 1902.

40. Quoted in DeVoto, *Journals*.

41. Quoted in DeVoto, *Journals*.

42. Quoted in Ewers, *The Adventures of Zenas Leonard*.

43. Quoted in Peter Nabokov, ed., *Native American Testimony*. New York: Viking, 1978.

44. Smith, *The Southwest Expeditions of Jedediah Smith*.

45. Quoted in Alter, *James Bridger*.

46. Quoted in Alter, *James Bridger*.

47. Quoted in David Weber, *The Taos Trappers*. Norman: University of Oklahoma Press, 1966.

48. Quoted in Kit Carson, *Kit Carson's Autobiography*. Lincoln: University of Nebraska Press, 1966.

49. Quoted in Carson, *Autobiography*.

50. Quoted in Nevins, *Fremont*.

51. Quoted in Charles Preuss, *Exploring with Fremont*. Norman: University of Oklahoma Press, 1958.

Chapter 6: The Other Enemies

52. Quoted in Mark Derr, *The Frontiersman*. New York: William Morrow, 1993.

53. Quoted in Derr, *The Frontiersman*.

54. Quoted in DeVoto, *Journals*.

55. Quoted in DeVoto, *Journals*.

56. Quoted in LeRoy Hafen, *Mountain Men and the Fur Trade in the Far West*. New York: Arthur H. Clark, 1965.

57. Quoted in Hafen, *Mountain Men*.

58. Quoted in Hafen, *Mountain Men*.

59. Quoted in Dale I. Morgan, *Jedediah Smith and the Opening of the West*. New York: Bobbs-Merrill, 1953.

60. Quoted in Morgan, *Jedediah Smith*.

61. Quoted in Morgan, *Jedediah Smith*.

62. Quoted in Ewers, *The Adventures of Zenas Leonard*.

63. Quoted in Cleland, *Reckless Breed*.

64. Quoted in Hafen, *Mountain Men*.

65. Quoted in Carson, *Autobiography*.

66. Quoted in Hafen, *Mountain Men*.

67. Quoted in Hafen, *Mountain Men*.

Chapter 7: The Great Battles

68. Quoted in Ray Allen Billington, *Westward Expansion*. New York: Macmillan, 1967.

69. Quoted in Stannard, *American Holocaust*.

70. Quoted in Stannard, *American Holocaust*.

71. Quoted in Bakeless, *Daniel Boone*.

72. Quoted in Bakeless, *Daniel Boone*.

73. Quoted in John D. Barnhart, *Henry Hamilton and George Rogers Clark in the American Revolution*. New York: R. E. Banta, 1951.

74. Quoted in Barnhart, *Henry Hamilton and George Rogers Clark*.

75. Quoted in Barnhart, *Henry Hamilton and George Rogers Clark*.

76. Quoted in Barnhart, *Henry Hamilton and George Rogers Clark*.

77. Quoted in Stannard, *American Holocaust*.

For Further Reading

Stephen E. Ambrose, *Undaunted Courage*. New York: Simon & Schuster, 1996. The best single-volume study of Lewis and Clark. Blends the high points of both Lewis's and Clark's personal journals with sharp and original observations. Reads like a historical novel. The reader comes to care very deeply about the characters, especially Meriwether Lewis, whose descent into suicide gradually overtakes the reader like a foreboding fog.

Thomas D. Clark, *Frontier America*. New York: Charles Scribner's Sons, 1969. Exhaustive yet highly readable overview of the entire subject. Chapters nicely broken down, making it easy for the reader to locate specific material. A good place for readers with a serious interest to start.

The Editors of American Heritage, *The American Heritage History of the Great West*. New York: American Heritage, 1965. Turn the pages of this one and treat yourself to a luxuriant stroll through the majesty and poignancy of the westward movement. The pictures and captions will entertain you. The scholarly yet approachable narrative will educate you.

Lawrence Elliot, *The Long Hunter*. New York: Reader's Digest Press, 1976. Fictional account of trailblazers in the mold of Daniel Boone. Full of historically accurate descriptions of food, clothing, and shelter of the lone Indian fighter. The reading level is intended to draw readers in and encourage them rather than intimidate them with excessive verbiage.

James T. Flexnor, *Doctors on Horseback*. New York: Dover Publications, 1969. Interesting look at the practice of frontier medicine. Moving in some parts, shocking in others. Many colorful anecdotes enliven the telling of this often overlooked aspect of the frontier.

Theodore Roosevelt, *The Winning of the West*. New York: Putnam's Sons, 1912. There have been many reprints of the multivolume classic. Once readers adjust to the somewhat archaic writing style, they will be treated to a rapid-paced adventure story, which just happens to relay the true facts (mostly) of the entire American migration west. Patriotic, inspiring, and remarkably respectful of the Indians. The reader enjoys the added advantage of becoming intimate with one of our most flamboyant presidents.

James Alexander Thom, *Follow the River*. New York: Ballantine Books, 1995. The compelling story of Mary Draper Ingles's harrowing journey in 1755 after being kidnapped by Shawnee Indians in Virginia (now West Virginia). No single book portrays the struggle for survival during the early settlement period better. Based on historical research, but written as fiction.

Works Consulted

Cecil Alter, *James Bridger*. New York: Shepard, 1955. Somewhat favorably biased account of Jim Bridger's life, but on the whole the author stays with the facts. Perhaps Bridger really was as good a man as Alter says. Maps and diagrams of the high points in Bridger's travels and escapades are helpful.

John Bakeless, *Daniel Boone*. New York: Stackpole, 1965. In-depth biography that pays particular attention to Boone's conflicts with the French, British, and, especially, the Indians. Scholarly but fast-paced and highly readable.

John D. Barnhart, *Henry Hamilton and George Rogers Clark in the American Revolution*. New York: R. E. Banta, 1951. All you ever wanted to know about the title characters. Climaxes with a detailed and dramatic retelling of the Battle of Vincennes. One of the first revisionist accounts that did not vilify Hamilton and deify Clark. Shows the strengths and weaknesses inherent in "great" and "terrible" men.

Ray Allen Billington, *Westward Expansion*. New York: Macmillan, 1967. Particularly helpful in describing relations between whites and Indians in the East. Boldly delineates battles, captures, murders, and torture. Uses understated quotations from the time to chillingly expose the brutality practiced by both sides.

Kit Carson, *Kit Carson's Autobiography*. Lincoln: University of Nebraska Press, 1966. Tells of the nearly unbelievable adventures that made him the most famous Indian fighter in the West from fighting braves to grizzly bears to sandstorms and blizzards. These are the stories that dime novelists blew into their absurd tall tales. They need not have. The truth as written here was sensational enough.

Hiram M. Chittendon, *The American Fur Trade of the Far West*. 3 vols. New York: F. P. Harper, 1902. Difficult to find in public library collections, but a fine resource when available in university libraries. Despite archaic language, author provides many heretofore forgotten or overlooked facts and anecdotes about the western trappers. Tends toward the academic, but readers willing to search it out and study it will be rewarded with many enlightening "nuggets."

Robert Cleland, *This Reckless Breed of Men*. New York: Knopf, 1952. Emphasizes the adventuresome spirit and rollicking deeds of the Indian fighters of the West. Unabashedly casts the frontiersmen as the good guys and the Indians as the bad. Revels in the mountain man spirit that cleared the way for the settlers. Refreshing in our present age of politically correct pioneer bashing.

H. L. Coles, *The War of 1812*. Chicago: University of Chicago Press, 1965. Comprehensive overview of one of the least popular wars in American history (the New England states almost seceded from the Union because they did not want to fight it). Particularly strong in its insights regarding the western states and their support. Clear maps and charts are helpful.

Daniel Conner, *Joseph Reddeford Walker*. Norman: University of Oklahoma Press, 1956. Scholarly account of one of the most important, yet overlooked, of the Indian fighters. Provides revealing psychological character of the "man who did not follow trails but made them." Also, explores some of the possible reasons why less accomplished men became famous while he did not.

R. E. Dabney, *Mountain Spirits*. New York: Charles Scribner's Sons, 1974. A light-hearted look at the mountain people and their beloved "likker" from the time of the Indian fighters to the present day. Contains recipes and instructions for the serious "re-enactor" and plenty of humorous anecdotes regarding stills, "revenuers," and those under the influence. Its main fault is that it tends to validate and perhaps promote drinking.

J. DeHass, *History of the Early Settlement and Indian Wars of West Virginia*. Parsons, WV: McClain, 1990. Stories of pioneers overcoming or succumbing to unspeakable hardships. Originally written in the 1840s, so the reader may find the archaic literary style distracting, this book offers a wealth of information. The author takes many of his stories directly from conversations with the actual white participants. As a result, this work has a decided anti-Indian bias.

Mark Derr, *The Frontiersman*. New York: William Morrow, 1993. Quickly becoming one of the most respected biographies of David Crockett, this book avoids mythologizing the frontiersman. In fact, the author forthrightly debuncts the particular myth that Crockett was a great soldier, choosing instead to venerate his political and self-promotional skills. Explores his most legitimate frontier achievement of ridding dangerous black bears from inhabited areas.

Bernard DeVoto, ed., *The Journals of Lewis and Clark*. New York: Houghton Mifflin, 1953. Edited and interwoven versions of both Lewis's and Clark's separately recorded journals of their legendary expedition. Includes only the high points of the journey, sparing the reader the enormous task of wading through the thousands of more mundane pages. Lets the great explorers speak for themselves.

Richard Dunlop, *Doctors of the American Frontier*. New York: Doubleday, 1965. Entertaining account of the beginnings of American medicine as seen through eyes of a physician. Leans more toward the human aspects of treating illness and injury on the frontier than the clinical ones although colorfully annotated footnotes expand upon the medical perspectives and refer the reader on to more scientific sources.

Allan W. Eckert, *That Dark and Bloody River*. New York: Bantam Books, 1995. Thoroughly researched history of the Ohio River valley during the eighteenth century. Author documents the daily struggles of the white Indian fighters and pioneers and the Indians whom they are attempting to displace. Spares the reader very little in describing the atrocious acts committed on both sides and supports the exciting narrative with an abundance of previously little known period quotes.

John C. Ewers, ed., *The Adventures of Zenas Leonard—Fur Trader*. Norman: University of Oklahoma Press, 1959. Zenas Leonard appears to have been everywhere and done everything with everyone in the Indian-fighting West. He not only lived to tell about it, but he wrote it all down in his journal, too. The result is one of the most colorful, adventuresome, and informative documents to come out of the period. And to cap it all off, Leonard maintains a rare and genuine sense of humility through it all. A national treasure.

John Filson, *The Discovery, Settlement, and Present State of Kentucke.* New York: Corinth Books, 1962. Contains the famous "autobiography" of Daniel Boone. Though Boone acknowledged that he had not actually written it, he swore that his dictation to Filson was accurate. As such, it provides the only work containing Boone's own recollections of his finest Indian-fighting days. Extraordinary.

Thomas Froncek, ed., *Voices from the Wilderness.* New York: McGraw-Hill, 1974. A collection of famous and not-so-famous people who lived in the eastern mountains during the colonial, Revolutionary War, and post-independence periods. Allows the characters to speak in their own words as they describe all facets of frontier life, including Indian fighting. A very helpful primary source.

Rupert Furneaux, *The Pictorial History of the American Revolution.* Chicago: J. G. Ferguson, 1973. In the style of the American Heritage pictorial histories. A delight to the eye and mind. Many paintings and sketches of battles, daily living, personages, and dwellings as well as a fast, instructional narrative throughout. Facts presented in small, digestible bites.

Arrel Morgan Gibson, *The American Indian.* Lexington, MA: D. C. Heath, 1980. Schol-arly work that adds significantly to the body of knowledge. Includes unexpected chapters on such topics as American Indians as the earliest pioneers, Indians in the Civil War (both as combatants and non-combatants), and the fate of Southern Indians during Reconstruction. Tedious reading but well worth the effort. Enhancing charts and notes.

LeRoy Hafen, *Mountain Men and the Fur Trade in the Far West.* New York: Arthur H. Clark, 1965. Full of stories, adventures, facts, and inspiration. Pays special attention to the courage, fortitude, and spirit of nearly every known mountain man. Good maps and sketches. Many descriptions of conflict with aggressive Indians and cooperation with those friendly to the whites.

William T. Hagan, *American Indians.* Chicago: University of Chicago Press, 1961. Helpful in that it treats the Indians not as one monolithic nation but as tribes varying from the warlike Sioux to the Papagos, who considered war a form of insanity. Interestingly pursues the concept that there was not an "average" type of white man either and that white behavior, while predominantly hostile, was not exclusively so. Offers a solid treatment of twentieth-century Indians as well. Thoroughly annotated suggested reading section and concise chronology of important dates from 1622 to 1958.

Jon P. Hale, *Trans-Allegheny Pioneers.* New York: Derreth, 1971. More stories of massacre, rape, murder, and the tenacity of the first white settlers to venture beyond the Appalachian Mountains. Significant for piecing together the story of Mary Ingles, who escaped from Indians in Ohio and somehow blazed her way back home to Virginia.

Wilber R. Jacobs, *Dispossessing the American Indian*. New York: Charles Scribner's Sons, 1972. Admirably pictures the clash of two cultures in a way that understands both these cultures, not just one. Focuses on an often neglected period in American Indian history: colonial and early U.S. In-depth annotated footnotes.

Albert N. Josephy Jr., *500 Nations*. New York: Knopf, 1994. American history from the American Indian point of view. Story of leaders, customs, political systems, and ways of life. Heavily biased in favor of the Indians and often needlessly critical of the whites but an indispensable aid, nonetheless, to understanding the experience of being Indian in America. Splendidly rich in maps, charts, photos, and art.

Richard C. Knopf, *Anthony Wayne*. Pittsburgh: University of Pittsburgh Press, 1959. Competent biography of the renowned general who "madly" helped to beat the British in the Revolutionary War and more cautiously defeated the Indians some twenty years later. Many illuminating quotes but not a particularly exciting read.

Harold Melton, *Jim Beckwourth, Negro Mountain Man*. New York: Dodd, Mead, 1970. An extremely colorful and entertaining biography simply because Jim Beckwourth was himself a colorful and entertaining person. He was flamboyant and self-aggrandizing, casting doubt on the veracity of some of his tales. However, if only when considering the escapades verified by the author, his is a life worth examining and this author examines it well.

Max Morehead, *The Commerce of the Prairie*. Norman: University of Oklahoma Press, 1963. A scholarly treatment of the economic conditions that developed among whites and between whites and Indians in the West. The author enhances a somewhat boring text with descriptions of medical practices, foods, and other aspects of daily life.

Dale I. Morgan, *Jedediah Smith and the Opening of the West*. New York: Bobbs-Merrill, 1953. One of the first books to introduce Smith to the American public. This now-legendary pathfinder had existed largely as a footnote in U.S. history before Morgan and a handful of others brought him to light. Most of the information included can now be found in more recent and, arguably, more readable accounts primarily because "modern" writers continue to rely on Morgan's ground-breaking research.

Peter Nabokov, ed., *Native American Testimony*. New York: Viking, 1978. American Indian history as told through quotations of American Indians themselves. Editor's narrative gives cohesion to the collection and a sense of the flow of the historical process in the tragic encounter of opposing values. Helpful maps and photographs.

Allan Nevins, *Fremont: Pathmarker of the West*. New York: Frederick, 1961. One of America's most respected historians and scholars takes on "the Great Pathfinder" with more generosity than more recent historians. He goes into perhaps more minute detail than many general readers would prefer, but the work is a masterpiece of research, writing, and insight nonetheless.

Grace C. Nute, *The Voyageurs*. St. Paul: Minnesota Historical Society, 1989. Emphasizes the role of the early French-Canadian fur trappers and their relationship with the Indians. The author offers a helpful comparison of the French-Canadian and English approaches to conducting business with the natives. Also delineates in great detail the everyday living conditions of the trappers themselves.

Charles Preuss, *Exploring with Fremont*. Norman: University of Oklahoma Press, 1958. Extraordinarily insightful memoirs of the German mapmaker who accompanied John C. Fremont. Particularly interesting in that he appears not to have respected or admired the "Great Pathfinder." Serves as a helpful counterweight to Fremont's own self-serving journals.

George Ruxton, *Ruxton of the Rockies*, ed. Mae Reed Porter and LeRoy R. Hafen. Norman: University of Oklahoma Press, 1950. Journal of a fur-trapping Indian fighter. Especially revealing regarding the Indian slave trade. Ruxton spends a great part of his narrative describing his everyday life. The adventure sometimes drags when he focuses on the mundane aspects of living, but the journal is valuable in that regard as a social history of the time and place.

Jedediah Smith, *The Southwest Expeditions of Jedediah Smith*. Lincoln: University of Nebraska Press, 1989. Smith describes in his own words the story of becoming the first white man to lead a party into California: the desert heat, the lack of water, and the hostile Indians. Also included are explanations of his tenuous relations with Spanish and Mexican officials who considered him a trespasser if not a spy. Offers a rare and illuminating glimpse into mission life in the Spanish Southwest.

Jared Stallones, *Zebulon Pike*. New York: Chelsea, 1976. A brief, readable account of the man who did so much more than discover a mountain. Daring in that it unblinkingly suggests that Pike had something to do with a conspiracy to break the West away from the United States and form a separate country, but responsibly does not off-handedly categorize him as a principal in the treason that never came to be. Much to learn about Pike here.

David E. Stannard, *American Holocaust*. New York: Oxford University Press, 1992. Exhaustively researched and documented study of the white man's inhumanity to the Indian. Vivid, relentless, and devastating portrait of death, disease, and genocide. Holds Christianity ultimately to blame for the extermination of a race. Gruesome yet effective descriptions of the endless cruelties. Nearly one hundred pages of appendices and notes. Condemning, infuriating, essential to understanding the anger of today's American Indians.

Irving Stone, *Men to Match My Mountains*. New York: Berkley Books, 1956. Perhaps the greatest historical novel of the West, certainly of the Far West. Contains a compelling, human story of the western migration with particular emphasis on the settling of California and the Oregon Territory. History breathes and bleeds in the hands of this literary master.

Raymond Thorp and Robert Bunker, *Crow Killer*. Bloomington: Indiana University Press, 1958. Oral tradition handed down to the authors concerning one of the most famous Indian fighters known in America today (due entirely to Hollywood): Jeremiah Johnson. Relies heavily upon the tales told by one of Johnson's friends and fellow trappers and can never be independently corroborated. However, the events contained therein are likely correct in essence. Either way, the book provides a colorful and revealing portrait of mountain life at the height of the trappers' era.

Edward Tunis, *Frontier Living*. New York: World Publishing, 1961. Rich in original drawings and text describing every aspect of daily life on the frontier from food to shelter to transportation. Compares the differences in habit and custom between people living on the deepwater frontier, the piedmont, the southern valleys, and the great salient (Kentucky and Tennessee). Also includes a general political and military history of the region.

David Weber, *The Taos Trappers*. Norman: University of Oklahoma Press, 1966. Emphasizes Kit Carson's contributions to settling the West for the white man. Offers many previously overlooked instances of Carson's savage affinity and ability for fighting Indians. Also amplifies lesser-knows trappers, explorers, and Indian fighters who based themselves out of Taos, New Mexico (then the most significant city in the Southwest). Fast-paced and entertaining reading for a scholarly work.

Index

Picture Credits

About the Author

James P. Reger grew up in Buckhannon, West Virginia, site of many Indian battles during the 1700s. Delaware braves captured one of his direct ancestors as a young girl and hatcheted her mother to death before her eyes. The girl lived on with the Indians in Ohio as a slave "wife" until released by treaty several years later. A roadside marker outside of Buckhannon commemorates the deeds of another ancestor who ran 125 miles in just twenty-four hours to warn the settlement of an impending Indian attack and then set up an ambush that routed the attackers.

For these reasons and many more, Reger has long thrilled to lore about frontiersmen and Indians battling for the land. He has even taken up buckskins and a flintlock on occasion to act the role in dramas and reenactments. It inspires him to reflect that he may still possess a bit of the genetic pedigree that made his ancestors so strong. Never one to take himself too seriously, he is fond of amusing himself with the thought, "If the pioneer Regers could endure all of the hardships that they did, then, surely, I can handle sixth period."

Reger now lives in San Diego, California, where he enjoys all of his passions: teaching, writing, and his wife and young son.